Microsoft
Word 2007
A Word Processing Software

Copyrighted © 2015 **John Monyjok Maluth**

*

ISBN: 9781520254210

*

Discipleship Press

Website: www.discipleshippress.wordpress.com
Email: maluthabiel@gmail.com
Phone: +254 110 424 822

~~*~~

P.O. Box 28448-00100, Nairobi Kenya

Library of Congress Control Number: 2022907818

All rights reserved. No part of this book may be reproduced, stored in a retrieval system, or transmitted in any or by any means – electronic, mechanical, photocopying, recording, or otherwise-without prior permission in writing from the copyright holder.

ABOUT THIS BOOK

This book teaches Microsoft Word 2007 from the ground up. It is written for beginners who want to type, format, and print clean documents without feeling lost in menus and buttons. You will learn the skills in the same order you actually need them: start a document, save it, fix mistakes, format it, insert images and tables, handle page numbers, and produce a final copy that looks professional.

WHO THIS BOOK IS FOR

This book is for you if:
You are new to Microsoft Word or you only know basic typing.
You want to write letters, school reports, church documents, CVs, meeting minutes, or simple business documents.
You want to stop fighting with spacing, page numbers, pictures that move around, and lists that break.

WHO THIS BOOK IS NOT FOR

This book is not meant for advanced users who already build complex templates, long legal documents with heavy automation, or professional publishing layouts every day. But if you are a beginner and you stay with the practice tasks, you will still reach strong, confident skills.

HOW THIS BOOK IS ORGANIZED

This book is divided into Parts and Chapters.
Each chapter teaches one clear skill set.
Each chapter ends with a small practice task you can complete in 5 to 20 minutes.
Later in the book, you will combine the skills into real projects like a one-page letter, a CV, and a school report.

HOW TO LEARN FAST WITH THIS BOOK

1. Read a chapter, then do the practice task immediately.

2. Type along in Word, do not only read.

3. Save your practice files in one folder so you can track your progress.

4. Do not rush formatting. Clean formatting is a skill, not a trick.

5. If something breaks, use Undo first. Then read the troubleshooting steps.

WHAT YOU NEED BEFORE YOU START
A computer with Microsoft Word 2007 installed.
A keyboard and mouse.
A place to save your files (Desktop, Documents folder, or a flash drive).
A printer is helpful, but not required. You can still learn by using Print Preview.
Optional but useful:
A small set of sample photos for practice (any pictures on your computer).
A simple list of names and addresses for mail merge practice.

YOUR PRACTICE FOLDER SETUP
Create one folder for all practice work.
Name it: Word 2007 Practice
Inside it, create these folders:
01 Quick Start
02 Writing Basics
03 Formatting
04 Page Setup
05 Insert Tools
06 Long Documents
07 Mail Merge
08 Review
09 Projects

Name your files clearly, like this:
Letter Practice 01
CV Practice 01
Report Practice 01

A Simple Daily Practice Plan
If you can study 15 minutes a day:
Day 1 to Day 3: Quick start, saving, printing basics
Day 4 to Day 8: Editing and formatting basics

Day 9 to Day 12: Page setup, headers, footers, page numbers
Day 13 to Day 16: Pictures, tables, shapes, simple layouts
Day 17 to Day 20: Headings and table of contents
Day 21 to Day 23: Mail merge basics
Day 24 to Day 26: Review tools, track changes
Day 27 to Day 30: Projects and troubleshooting

Common Terms You Must Know

Document
A file you create in Word, like a letter or report.

Cursor (Insertion Point)
The blinking line where your next typing will appear.

Ribbon
The top area in Word 2007 that contains tabs and command buttons.

Tab
A category on the Ribbon, like Home or Insert.

Group
A section inside a tab that holds related tools, like Font or Paragraph.

Dialog Box Launcher
A small arrow in the corner of some groups that opens more settings.

Office Button
The round button in the top-left corner of Word 2007. It is where you create, open, save, print, and close files.

Quick Access Toolbar
Small icons near the top-left for common actions like Save and Undo.

Status Bar
The bar at the bottom that shows page number, word count, view buttons, and zoom.

Template
A ready-made document design you can reuse, like a resume layout.

Formatting
How your text looks: font, size, spacing, alignment, and layout.

Style
A preset set of formatting that keeps your document consistent, especially for headings.

Page Break
A command that forces text to start on a new page.

Section Break
A break that allows different page settings in the same document, like different headers or page numbering.

Header and Footer
Text that repeats at the top and bottom of pages, like a title or page number.

Contextual Tabs
Extra tabs that appear only when you select an object, like a picture or a table.

File Types: .doc and .docx
.doc is the older Word format.
.docx is the newer Word format used by Word 2007 by default.

A Quick Promise to the Beginner
If you practice consistently, you will stop guessing. You will know what to click, why you are clicking it, and how to fix problems when something looks wrong.

CONTENTS

PART I: QUICK START FOR ABSOLUTE BEGINNERS 1

    CHAPTER 1: WHAT MICROSOFT WORD 2007 IS AND WHAT YOU CAN DO WITH IT 1

    CHAPTER 2: THE WORD 2007 SCREEN TOUR 4

    CHAPTER 3: CREATE, SAVE, AND REOPEN DOCUMENTS 7

    CHAPTER 4: PRINT BASICS WITHOUT WASTING PAPER 10

PART II: WRITING AND EDITING BASICS 13

    CHAPTER 1: TYPING, MOVING THE CURSOR, AND SELECTING TEXT 13

    CHAPTER 2: UNDO, REDO, AND FIXING MISTAKES FAST 16

    CHAPTER 3: CUT, COPY, PASTE, AND THE CLIPBOARD 19

    CHAPTER 4: FIND AND REPLACE FOR BEGINNERS 23

CHAPTER PART III: CLEAN FORMATTING THAT LOOKS PROFESSIONAL 26

    CHAPTER 1: FONTS MADE SIMPLE 26

    CHAPTER 2: PARAGRAPH FORMATTING THAT ACTUALLY MATTERS 29

    CHAPTER 3: BULLETS, NUMBERING, AND MULTILEVEL LISTS 33

    CHAPTER 4: STYLES FOR BEGINNERS 37

    CHAPTER 5: FORMAT PAINTER AND CLEARING FORMATTING .. 41

PART IV: PAGE SETUP AND DOCUMENT LAYOUT 45

    CHAPTER 1: PAGE SETUP BASICS 45

    CHAPTER 2: PAGE BREAKS AND SECTION BREAKS 49

    CHAPTER 3: HEADERS, FOOTERS, AND PAGE NUMBERS 53

    CHAPTER 4: COLUMNS AND PAGE BACKGROUND TOOLS 57

PART V: INSERT TOOLS YOU WILL USE OFTEN (INSERT TAB) 61

    CHAPTER 1: PICTURES DONE RIGHT 61

    CHAPTER 2: SHAPES, TEXT BOXES, AND WORDART 65

    CHAPTER 3: TABLES FOR BEGINNERS 69

    CHAPTER 4: SMARTART AND CHARTS 74

    CHAPTER 5: SYMBOLS AND EQUATIONS (BASIC USE) 78

PART VI: REFERENCES AND ACADEMIC WORK (REFERENCES TAB) 82

CHAPTER 1: HEADINGS THAT MAKE LONG DOCUMENTS EASY .82
CHAPTER 2: TABLE OF CONTENTS THE CORRECT WAY 87
CHAPTER 3: FOOTNOTES AND ENDNOTES 91
CHAPTER 4: CITATIONS AND BIBLIOGRAPHY BASICS................94
CHAPTER 5: CAPTIONS AND CROSS-REFERENCES 98
CHAPTER 6: INDEX AND TABLE OF AUTHORITIES (OPTIONAL) 102

PART VII: PAGE LAYOUT TOOLS (PAGE LAYOUT TAB) 106

CHAPTER 1: THEMES AND BASIC DOCUMENT LOOK 106
CHAPTER 2: INDENTS, SPACING, AND LAYOUT CONTROLS 110
CHAPTER 3: PAGE BORDERS AND WATERMARK FOR OFFICIAL DOCUMENTS...115

PART VIII: MAILINGS FOR BEGINNERS (MAILINGS TAB)...........119

CHAPTER 1: ENVELOPES AND LABELS 119
CHAPTER 2: MAIL MERGE STEP BY STEP 123
CHAPTER 3: CLEANING RECIPIENT LISTS...................................128

PART IX: REVIEW TOOLS (REVIEW TAB)....................................132

CHAPTER 1: SPELLING AND GRAMMAR TOOLS 132
CHAPTER 2: COMMENTS FOR FEEDBACK 136
CHAPTER 3: TRACK CHANGES FOR EDITING 140
CHAPTER 4: COMPARE AND COMBINE DOCUMENTS 144
CHAPTER 5: PROTECTING A DOCUMENT 148

PART X: VIEW AND NAVIGATION (VIEW TAB) 152

CHAPTER 1: VIEWS EXPLAINED 152
CHAPTER 2: ZOOM, SPLIT, AND SIDE-BY-SIDE READING..........157
CHAPTER 3: SHOW/HIDE MARKS TO FIX MESSY DOCUMENTS 161

PART XI: THE HIDDEN TOOLS (CONTEXTUAL TABS) 165

CHAPTER 1: WHAT CONTEXTUAL TABS ARE 165
CHAPTER 2: TABLE TOOLS (DESIGN AND LAYOUT) 169
CHAPTER 3: PICTURE TOOLS (FORMAT) 174
CHAPTER 4: DRAWING TOOLS FOR SHAPES AND TEXT BOXES 178
CHAPTER 5: HEADER AND FOOTER TOOLS 182

PART XII: BEGINNER PROJECTS (REWRITE THE BOOK BY BUILDING REAL DOCUMENTS) 186

CHAPTER 1: PROJECT 1: A ONE-PAGE LETTER..........................186
CHAPTER 2: PROJECT 2: A SIMPLE CV 190

CHAPTER 3: PROJECT 3: A SCHOOL REPORT 195
CHAPTER 4: PROJECT 4: A FLYER OR ANNOUNCEMENT 200
CHAPTER 5: TROUBLESHOOTING CLINIC 205

BACK MATTER 210

PART I: QUICK START FOR ABSOLUTE BEGINNERS

CHAPTER 1: WHAT MICROSOFT WORD 2007 IS AND WHAT YOU CAN DO WITH IT

What Microsoft Word 2007 is

Microsoft Word 2007 is a word processing program. It helps you create documents, edit them easily, format them neatly, save them, share them, and print them.

What you can do with Word 2007 as a beginner

Write documents
- Letters
- School assignments
- Meeting minutes
- Reports
- Simple manuscripts

Edit without starting over
- Insert missing sentences
- Delete repeated lines
- Move paragraphs up or down
- Fix spelling mistakes quickly

Make your work look professional
- Control fonts and font sizes
- Control spacing and alignment
- Set margins and page layout
- Add headings and page numbers

Insert useful items
- Pictures
- Tables
- Shapes
- Symbols
- Simple charts

Prepare for printing
- Preview pages before printing
- Print only what you need
- Reduce printing errors and wasted paper

What Word 2007 is not

Word 2007 is not a graphic design tool. It can create clean, good-looking documents, but its main job is writing, editing, and clear page formatting.

Where Word 2007 is used most
- Students: assignments and research papers
- Offices: letters, minutes, proposals, reports
- Small businesses: simple forms and announcements
- Authors: drafting and editing manuscripts

The main idea to remember
Word has two main jobs:
- Help you write and edit words easily
- Help you present those words clearly on a page

Practice Example (About 5 minutes)
Goal: Open Word, recognize where you type, and write one sentence.
Do this:
- Open Microsoft Word 2007
    o Click Start
    o Find Microsoft Office
    o Click Microsoft Office Word 2007
- Identify the blank document area
    o Look for the large white page in the middle
    o This is where you type
    o The blinking line is the cursor (your typing point)
- Type one sentence
    o Click once on the white page if needed
    o Type:
    I am learning Microsoft Word 2007.
- Save your practice file
    o Click the Office Button (top-left)
    o Click **Save As**
    o Choose **Word Document**
    o Name it: **Word Practice 01**
    o Save it inside your **Word 2007 Practice** folder

Quick check (self-test)
Ask yourself:
- What is Word 2007 used for?

- Where do you type?
- What is the cursor?
- How do you save a file?

CHAPTER 2: THE WORD 2007 SCREEN TOUR

This chapter helps you recognize the main parts of the Word 2007 screen, so you always know where you are and what you are clicking.

1) The Document Area (Where You Type)
This is the large white page in the center of the screen.
Everything you type appears here.
Tip: If you do not see the blinking cursor, click once on the white page.

2) The Ribbon (Your Main Tool Area)
The Ribbon is the wide strip across the top of Word.
It holds almost all the commands you will use.
Think of it like a toolbox that is organized into categories.

3) Tabs (Categories on the Ribbon)
Tabs are the names along the top of the Ribbon.
When you click a tab, you see its tools.
Common tabs you will use a lot:
- Home
- Insert
- Page Layout
- References
- Mailings
- Review
- View

4) Groups (Tool Sections Inside a Tab)
Inside each tab, tools are arranged in groups.
Example (Home tab groups):
- Clipboard
- Font
- Paragraph
- Styles
- Editing

Groups keep related tools together so you do not waste time searching.

5) Dialog Box Launchers (More Settings Button)

Some groups have a tiny arrow in the bottom-right corner.
That arrow is the Dialog Box Launcher.
When you click it, Word opens a bigger settings window with more options.
Example:
In the Font group, it opens the full Font settings box.
In the Paragraph group, it opens full paragraph settings.

6) The Office Button (File Commands)
The Office Button is the round button in the top-left corner.
This is where you go to:
- New
- Open
- Save
- Save As
- Print
- Close

If you forget where to save or print, start here.

7) Quick Access Toolbar (Your Shortcut Icons)
This is a small set of icons near the Office Button.
It usually includes:
- Save
- Undo
- Redo

You can add more shortcuts later, but as a beginner, these three are enough.

8) The Status Bar (Information Bar at the Bottom)
The Status Bar is the bar at the bottom of Word.
It commonly shows:
- Page number (Page 1 of 3)
- Word count
- Language
- View buttons
- Zoom slider

This bar helps you confirm what is happening in your document.

Practice Example (5 to 10 minutes)

Goal: Point to each area and name it out loud.
Do this in order:
1. Point to the white page and say: "Document area."
2. Point to the top tool strip and say: "Ribbon."
3. Point to the tab names and say: "Tabs."
4. Click Home, then point to sections like Font and say: "Groups."
5. Find the small arrow in a group and say: "Dialog Box Launcher."
6. Point to the round button and say: "Office Button."
7. Point to the small icons near it and say: "Quick Access Toolbar."
8. Point to the bottom bar and say: "Status Bar."

Quick check (self-test)
- Where do you go to Save As and Print?
- What do tabs do?
- What are groups?
- What does the Status Bar tell you?

CHAPTER 3: CREATE, SAVE, AND REOPEN DOCUMENTS

In this chapter, you will learn how to create a document, save it properly, and reopen it later without losing your work.

1) Create a New Document
Option A: Start a new document when Word opens
Most of the time, Word opens with a blank document already ready.
Option B: Create a new document from inside Word
1. Click the **Office Button** (top-left).
2. Click **New**.
3. Choose **Blank document**.
4. Click **Create**.

2) Save vs Save As (Know the Difference)
Save
Use **Save** when:
- You already named the file before.
- You want to update the same file with new changes.

Shortcut:
- Press **Ctrl + S** often.

Save As
Use **Save As** when:
- You want to name the file for the first time.
- You want to create a second copy with a different name.
- You want to save in a different location or file type.

3) File Locations (Where Your Document Is Stored)
When you save, Word puts your file into a folder on your computer.
Common locations beginners use:
- **Desktop** (easy to find quickly)
- **Documents** (best for organized storage)
- **A flash drive** (portable, but can be lost easily)

Important habit:
- Always know where you are saving before you click Save.

4) File Types: .doc vs .docx (Simple Explanation)

.docx
- The default format in Word 2007.
- Works best with Word 2007 and newer versions.

.doc
- The older Word format (from Word 2003 and earlier).
- Useful if you must share with someone using older Word versions.

Beginner rule:
- Use **.docx** unless you have a clear reason to use **.doc**.

Practice Example (10 minutes)
Goal: Create "My Practice.docx", save to Desktop, close it, and reopen it.

Step 1: Create the file
1. Open Word 2007.
2. If you see a blank page, you already have a new document.

Step 2: Type something small
Type this line:
This is my first saved practice file in Word 2007.

Step 3: Save it to Desktop
1. Click the **Office Button**.
2. Click **Save As**.
3. Choose **Word Document**.
4. In the location area, choose **Desktop**.
5. File name: **My Practice**
6. Click **Save**.

Quick check:
- Look at the top of Word. The file name should now show **My Practice**.

Step 4: Close the document
1. Click the **Office Button**.
2. Click **Close**.
   If Word asks to save changes, click **Save**.

Step 5: Reopen the document
Option A (from Desktop):
1. Go to your Desktop.
2. Double-click **My Practice.docx**.

Option B (from Word):
1. Open Word 2007.

2. Click the **Office Button**.
3. Click **Open**.
4. Select **My Practice.docx** on Desktop.
5. Click **Open**.

Common Beginner Problems (Quick Fixes)

"I saved it, but I cannot find it."

Most likely causes:
- You saved it in **Documents** instead of Desktop.
- You saved it in a folder you did not notice.

Fix:
- Use Windows search and type: **My Practice**.

"Word keeps asking me to save again."

Cause:
- You are closing without saving changes.

Fix:
- Press **Ctrl + S** before you close.

Quick check (self-test)
- What is the difference between Save and Save As?
- Where did you save your practice file?
- Which file type is the default in Word 2007?
- How do you reopen a file from inside Word?

CHAPTER 4: PRINT BASICS WITHOUT WASTING PAPER

Printing becomes easy when you follow one rule: preview first, then print only what you need. This chapter shows you how to check your pages before you waste paper.

1) Print Preview (Always Check Before Printing)
Print Preview shows you exactly how your document will look on paper.
How to open Print Preview
 1. Click the **Office Button** (top-left).
 2. Point to **Print**.
 3. Click **Print Preview**.
What to look for in Print Preview:
- Is the text cut off at the edges?
- Are margins too small or too big?
- Are page numbers placed correctly?
- Does the document unexpectedly become 2 or 3 pages?

Tip: Many beginner printing problems are visible here before you print.

2) Page Count (Know How Many Pages You Will Print)
Quick ways to check page count
Option A: Use the Status Bar (bottom of Word)
- You will see something like: **Page 1 of 2**

Option B: Check in Print Preview
- It shows how many pages your document has as you scroll.

Why this matters:
- If you think you are printing 1 page but it is actually 3 pages, you waste paper.

3) Printer Selection (Choose the Right Printer)
When you click Print, Word lets you choose the printer. This is important if:
- You have more than one printer installed.
- You are in an office with shared printers.
- You sometimes use PDF printers (like "Microsoft XPS Document Writer").

Rule for beginners:

- Confirm the printer name before printing.

4) Print One Page First (Safe Printing Habit)
Before printing a full document, print one test page.
You do this when:
- You are unsure about margins, layout, or page numbering.
- You are using a printer you do not trust.
- You are printing an important document.

Practice Example (10 minutes)
Goal: Preview your document, then print a single test page.
Use your file from Chapter 3 (My Practice.docx), or create a short page of text.

Step 1: Open your practice file
- Open **My Practice.docx**

Step 2: Open Print Preview
1. Click the **Office Button**.
2. Point to **Print**.
3. Click **Print Preview**.

Step 3: Check the page count
Look for:
- "Page 1 of 1" or "Page 1 of 2" (exact wording may vary by view)

If you see more pages than expected:
- Look for extra blank lines at the end.
- Look for a page break you did not mean to add.

Step 4: Exit Print Preview
- Click **Close Print Preview** (usually on the Ribbon in preview mode)

Step 5: Print one page only
1. Click the **Office Button**.
2. Point to **Print**.
3. Click **Print**.
4. In the Page range section, choose **Pages**.
5. Type: **1**
6. Confirm the correct printer is selected.
7. Click **OK**.

Common Beginner Mistakes (And Fixes)

"It printed an extra blank page."
Most common causes:
- Extra paragraph marks (empty lines) at the end
- A page break inserted by mistake

Fix:
- Press **Ctrl + End** to jump to the end of the document.
- Delete extra blank lines.
- Use Print Preview again.

"The printer printed the wrong pages."
Cause:
- You did not set the page range.

Fix:
- Always choose **Pages** and type the page number for test prints.

"Nothing printed."
Possible causes:
- Wrong printer selected
- Printer is offline or out of paper
- Cable or network problem

Fix:
- Recheck printer selection first.
- Then check printer power, paper, and connection.

Quick check (self-test)
- Why should you always use Print Preview first?
- Where do you see the page count?
- How do you print only page 1?
- What is the safest way to test-print a document?

PART II: WRITING AND EDITING BASICS
CHAPTER 1: TYPING, MOVING THE CURSOR, AND SELECTING TEXT

This chapter teaches the three beginner skills that make Word feel easy: type confidently, move the cursor fast, and select text correctly.

1) Typing Basics (What Beginners Must Know)
The cursor (insertion point)
The cursor is the blinking line in your document.
Whatever you type appears where the cursor is blinking.
New lines vs new paragraphs
- Press **Enter** to start a new paragraph.
- Press **Shift + Enter** to start a new line without starting a new paragraph (useful in addresses).

Beginner rule:
Use **Enter** for real paragraph breaks. Do not press Enter many times to create space. You will learn clean spacing later.

2) Moving the Cursor With the Mouse (Simple and Fast)
Mouse movement is quick for short distances:
- Click once to place the cursor at a point in the text.
- Double-click a word to select it.
- Triple-click inside a paragraph to select the whole paragraph.

Scroll tip:
Use the mouse wheel to scroll.
Click in the text after scrolling to place the cursor.

3) Moving the Cursor With the Keyboard (Faster for Real Work)
Keyboard movement is best when you want precision.
Basic movement keys
- Arrow keys: move one character or one line at a time
- **Ctrl + Left Arrow / Ctrl + Right Arrow**: jump word by word
- **Home**: jump to the start of the current line
- **End**: jump to the end of the current line
- **Ctrl + Home**: jump to the start of the document
- **Ctrl + End**: jump to the end of the document

- **Page Up / Page Down**: move by screen pages

4) Selecting Text (The Skill That Prevents Mistakes)
Selection means highlighting text so you can format it, delete it, move it, or copy it.

Selecting with the mouse
- Drag across text to select it
- Double-click to select one word
- Triple-click to select a whole paragraph

Selecting with the keyboard
- Hold **Shift** and use the Arrow keys to select little by little
- **Shift + Ctrl + Left/Right Arrow**: select one word at a time
- **Shift + Home**: select from the cursor to the start of the line
- **Shift + End**: select from the cursor to the end of the line
- **Ctrl + A**: select the entire document

Beginner warning:
If you type while text is selected, your typing replaces the selected text. This is one of the most common beginner accidents.

Practice Example (10 to 15 minutes)
Goal: Type 3 paragraphs, then select and highlight paragraph 2.

Step 1: Create a new document
1. Open Word 2007.
2. Use a blank document.

Step 2: Type three short paragraphs
Type this exactly, pressing **Enter** once after each paragraph.
Paragraph 1:
Today I am learning how to type and move around in Microsoft Word 2007. I want to become confident using the keyboard and mouse.
Paragraph 2:
Selecting text is important because it helps me edit and format my work quickly. If I select the wrong text, I may change something by mistake.

Paragraph 3:
With practice, I will move faster, make fewer errors, and write documents that look clean and professional.

Step 3: Select paragraph 2

Option A (easy mouse method):
1. Move your pointer into paragraph 2.
2. Triple-click inside that paragraph.

Option B (drag method):
1. Click at the start of paragraph 2.
2. Hold the left mouse button and drag to the end of paragraph 2.

Step 4: Highlight paragraph 2
1. With paragraph 2 still selected, go to the **Home** tab.
2. Find the **Text Highlight Color** tool (it looks like a marker).
3. Click it and choose **Yellow**.

Quick check (self-test)
- What does the cursor show you?
- What happens if you type while text is selected?
- How do you select a whole paragraph quickly?
- What does Ctrl + A do?

CHAPTER 2: UNDO, REDO, AND FIXING MISTAKES FAST

This chapter teaches the fastest way to recover from mistakes in Word 2007. If you master Undo and Redo, you will stop being afraid to try things.

1) Undo (Your Safety Button)
What Undo does
Undo reverses your most recent action.
Examples of actions you can undo:
- typing text
- deleting text
- formatting (bold, font size, color)
- moving text
- inserting an object

How to Undo
- Click the **Undo** icon on the Quick Access Toolbar (top-left), or
- Press **Ctrl + Z**

Undo history
In Word 2007, Undo works step-by-step.
You can press Undo multiple times to go back through your recent actions.
Beginner rule:
If something goes wrong, try **Ctrl + Z** first.

2) Redo (Bring Back What You Undid)
What Redo does
Redo restores an action you just undid.
Example:
- You undo a bold format by mistake
- Redo brings the bold back

How to Redo
- Click the **Redo** icon on the Quick Access Toolbar, or
- Press **Ctrl + Y**

Important:
Redo only works if the last thing you did was Undo.
If you do a new action after Undo, Redo may change into "Repeat" instead.

3) Repeat (Do the Same Action Again Quickly)

What Repeat does
Repeat repeats your last action.
Example:
- You made one line bold
- Repeat can make the next selected line bold without clicking Bold again

How to Repeat
- Press **Ctrl + Y** (often used for Redo or Repeat depending on what you did last)

Beginner tip:
Think of Ctrl + Y as:
- Redo if you just undid something
- Repeat if you did not undo anything

4) Fixing Mistakes Fast (A Simple Order)
When you make a mistake, do this in order:
1. Undo (Ctrl + Z)
2. Undo again if needed
3. If you undid too much, Redo (Ctrl + Y)
4. If you want to apply the same action again, use Repeat (Ctrl + Y)

Practice Example (10 minutes)
Goal: Apply bold, undo it, redo it, then repeat the action on another line.

Step 1: Type two lines
Type this exactly, pressing Enter once between lines:
Line 1:
Microsoft Word 2007 helps me write clearly.
Line 2:
Undo and Redo help me fix mistakes fast.

Step 2: Make Line 1 bold
1. Select Line 1 (drag across the sentence).
2. Press **Ctrl + B** (or click **Bold** on the Home tab).

Step 3: Undo the bold
- Press **Ctrl + Z**
  Line 1 should return to normal text.

Step 4: Redo the bold
- Press **Ctrl + Y**
  Line 1 should become bold again.

Step 5: Repeat the action on Line 2
   1. Select Line 2.
   2. Press **Ctrl + Y**

Expected result:
Line 2 should become bold without you clicking Bold again.
If it does not work:
- Apply bold to Line 2 using Ctrl + B once
- Then try Repeat again on another line to confirm the behavior

Common beginner problems (quick fixes)
"Undo removed something I did not mean to remove."
Fix:
- Press **Ctrl + Y** to redo.

"Redo is not working."
Cause:
- You performed a new action after Undo.

Fix:
- Undo again if needed, or manually reapply the formatting.

"Ctrl + Y did something different."
Reason:
- Ctrl + Y can act as Redo or Repeat depending on what happened last.

Fix:
- Use it carefully and watch what changes on the page.

Quick check (self-test)
- What is the keyboard shortcut for Undo?
- What is the keyboard shortcut for Redo or Repeat?
- When does Ctrl + Y act like Repeat?
- What should you try first when something goes wrong?

CHAPTER 3: CUT, COPY, PASTE, AND THE CLIPBOARD

This chapter teaches you how to move text safely, duplicate text quickly, and control what happens to formatting when you paste.

1) The Big Difference: Cut vs Copy

Cut (move text)

Cut removes text from one place so you can place it somewhere else.

Shortcut:
- **Ctrl + X**

Use Cut when:
- You typed a paragraph in the wrong place
- You want to move a sentence to a different section

Copy (duplicate text)

Copy keeps the original text and creates a duplicate you can paste elsewhere.

Shortcut:
- **Ctrl + C**

Use Copy when:
- You want the same paragraph in two places
- You want to reuse a standard message (address, signature, template text)

2) Paste (Place the Text)

Paste inserts what you cut or copied.

Shortcut:
- **Ctrl + V**

Beginner warning:

If you paste without checking formatting, your document can become messy. Word 2007 gives you paste options to control this.

3) The Clipboard (Where Word Holds What You Copy)

The clipboard is a temporary holding area for text and objects you cut or copy.

Important:
- You can copy something, then paste it many times.
- If you copy something new, it replaces what you copied before (for simple clipboard use).

4) Paste Options (The Key to Clean Documents)
After you paste, Word often shows a small paste icon near the pasted text.
That icon lets you choose how the pasted text should look.
Common paste choices you will see:
- Keep Source Formatting
- Match Destination Formatting
- Keep Text Only

Keep Source Formatting
The pasted text keeps the original font, size, spacing, and style.
Use this when:
- You are pasting into a document that uses the same formatting
- You want the pasted text to look exactly like it did before

Match Destination Formatting
The pasted text changes to match the formatting of where you pasted it.
Use this when:
- You are pasting from another document or website
- You want everything to look consistent

Keep Text Only
Word pastes only the words, removing most formatting.
Use this when:
- You copied from the internet or a messy document
- You want a clean paste with no strange fonts or spacing

Beginner rule:
If your document starts looking mixed and messy, use Match Destination or Keep Text Only more often.

Practice Example (10 to 15 minutes)
Goal: Copy one paragraph and paste it three ways.
Step 1: Create a new document
Open Word 2007 and use a blank page.
Step 2: Type two different formatted lines (so you can see the effect)
1. Type this title on the first line:
   My Practice Test

2. Make the title larger (example: size 16) and bold.
3. Press Enter and type this paragraph exactly:

Microsoft Word 2007 helps beginners create clean documents. Copy and paste saves time, but paste options help you control formatting.

Step 3: Copy the paragraph
1. Select the paragraph (drag across it).
2. Press **Ctrl + C**

Step 4: Paste it three ways

Paste 1: Normal paste (default)
1. Click at the end of the paragraph.
2. Press Enter once.
3. Press **Ctrl + V**
   This is your first paste.

Paste 2: Keep Source Formatting vs Match Destination
1. Press Enter once again.
2. Press **Ctrl + V** again.
3. Look for the small paste options icon.
4. Click it and choose **Match Destination Formatting**.

Paste 3: Keep Text Only
1. Press Enter once again.
2. Press **Ctrl + V** again.
3. Click the paste options icon.
4. Choose **Keep Text Only**.

What you should notice:
- One version may keep the original look
- Another version may match the surrounding style
- The "text only" version usually looks the cleanest when copying from messy sources

Extra skill (optional, but useful)
Try this:
- Copy a sentence from a website, paste it into Word, then choose **Keep Text Only**.
  This will show you why Word sometimes brings strange fonts and spacing.

Common beginner problems (quick fixes)
"My pasted text looks different from the rest of the document."

Fix:
- Use **Match Destination Formatting** or **Keep Text Only**.

"My pasted text brought strange spacing or weird font."
Fix:
- Paste again, then choose **Keep Text Only**.

"I accidentally removed text when I meant to copy it."
Fix:
- Press **Ctrl + Z** (Undo).

Quick check (self-test)
- What is the shortcut for Cut?
- What is the shortcut for Copy?
- What is the shortcut for Paste?
- Which paste option keeps your document consistent?

CHAPTER 4: FIND AND REPLACE FOR BEGINNERS

Find and Replace is one of the fastest tools in Word 2007. It helps you locate words instantly and fix repeated mistakes across a page or an entire document.

1) What Find Does

Find searches for a word or phrase in your document and takes you to each match.

Use Find when:
- You want to locate a name, date, or paragraph quickly
- You want to check where a word appears
- You want to review repeated terms

2) What Replace Does

Replace searches for a word or phrase and swaps it with another word or phrase.

Use Replace when:
- You typed a word wrongly many times
- You want to change a term throughout a document
- You want consistent wording (example: changing "report" to "paper")

3) Replace vs Replace All (Know When to Use Each)

Replace (one-by-one)

Replace changes one match at a time.

Use Replace when:
- You want to confirm each change
- The word might have different meanings in different places

Replace All (everywhere at once)

Replace All changes every match in the selected area (or entire document) immediately.

Use Replace All when:
- You are 100% sure every change is correct
- The word is clearly the same in every case

Beginner rule:
Start with Replace (one-by-one) until you trust your search term.

4) Safe Habits (So You Do Not Break Your Document)

Habit 1: Save before big replacements
Before using Replace All, press **Ctrl + S**.
Habit 2: Watch out for partial-word mistakes
If you replace "Word" with "Microsoft Word," it is fine.
But if you replace "or" with "and," you will ruin many words (like "work" becomes "wandk").
Rule:
Only replace meaningful words or phrases, not tiny pieces of words.
Habit 3: Use Replace All carefully
Replace All is powerful. One click can change hundreds of places.
If you are unsure:
- Use Replace, check a few, then continue

5) How to Open Find and Replace
Method A (fast keyboard method)
- Press **Ctrl + F** for Find
- Press **Ctrl + H** for Replace

Method B (from the Ribbon)
1. Click the **Home** tab
2. In the **Editing** group, click **Find** or **Replace**

Practice Example (10 minutes)
Goal: Replace "Word" with "Microsoft Word" in a page.
Step 1: Type a short practice page
Create a new document and type this text exactly (one paragraph is fine):
Word is useful for writing letters. Word is also useful for school work. When I learn Word well, I can prepare documents faster. Word has tools for editing and formatting.
Step 2: Open Replace
- Press **Ctrl + H**

Step 3: Fill the Replace box
In the dialog box:
- In **Find what,** type: Word
- In **Replace with,** type: Microsoft Word

Step 4: Choose how to replace
Option A (safe method: Replace one-by-one)
1. Click **Find Next**

2. When Word highlights "Word," click **Replace**
3. Repeat until you reach the end
4. When Word says it is finished, click **OK**

Option B (fast method: Replace All)
1. Click **Replace All**
2. Word will tell you how many replacements were made
3. Click **OK**

Step 5: Review your paragraph
Your text should now read:
Microsoft Word is useful for writing letters. Microsoft Word is also useful for school work. When I learn Microsoft Word well, I can prepare documents faster. Microsoft Word has tools for editing and formatting.

Common beginner problems (quick fixes)
"Replace All changed something I did not want."
Fix:
- Press **Ctrl + Z** immediately (Undo), then use Replace one-by-one.

"It did not find anything."
Possible causes:
- You typed "word" instead of "Word" (case difference)
- There is extra space in your search term

Fix:
- Recheck spelling and spacing, then try again.

"It replaced part of another word."
Cause:
- Your search term was too short or too general

Fix:
- Use full words and phrases only.

Quick check (self-test)
- What does Find do?
- What does Replace do?
- Why is Replace safer than Replace All for beginners?
- What shortcut opens Replace?

CHAPTER PART III: CLEAN FORMATTING THAT LOOKS PROFESSIONAL

CHAPTER 1: FONTS MADE SIMPLE

Fonts control how your words look. In Word 2007, clean font choices make your document easier to read and more professional.

1) Where Font Tools Are Found
Most font tools are in:
- **Home tab**
- **Font group**

You will use this group almost every time you write.

2) Font Type (The Style of Letters)
A font type is the design of the letters.
Examples:
- Times New Roman
- Calibri
- Arial

Beginner rule:
Choose one clear font and stay with it for the whole document unless you have a reason to change.

3) Font Size (How Big the Letters Are)
Font size controls readability.
Simple beginner guide:
- Titles: 16 to 20
- Headings: 14 to 16
- Normal text: 11 to 12

Beginner rule:
Do not mix many sizes. Two or three sizes are enough for most documents.

4) Bold, Italic, Underline (Basic Emphasis)
Bold
Makes text darker and heavier.
Use it for titles, headings, and key words.
Shortcut: **Ctrl + B**
Italic

Slants text slightly.
Use it for book titles, foreign words, or gentle emphasis.
Shortcut: **Ctrl + I**
Underline
Draws a line under text.
Use it rarely. Beginners often overuse underline.
Shortcut: **Ctrl + U**
Beginner rule:
If you need emphasis, choose bold or italic before underline.

5) Font Color (Use With Care)
Font color changes the color of text.
Use color when:
- You are creating a flyer or a learning worksheet
- You want a small highlight (not the whole page)

Beginner rule:
For letters, reports, and school work, keep text black unless the document requires color.

6) Change Case (Uppercase and Lowercase)
Word can change how letters appear without retyping.
Common case options:
- lowercase
- UPPERCASE
- Sentence case
- Capitalize Each Word

Where to find it:
- Home tab
- Font group
- The **Change Case** button (Aa)

Beginner rule:
Do not type whole paragraphs in ALL CAPS. It is harder to read.

7) The Safe Way to Apply Font Formatting
Always do this order:
1. Select the text you want to change
2. Apply the font tool (size, bold, color, etc.)

If you apply formatting without selecting text, Word formats what you type next instead.

Practice Example (10 minutes)
Goal: Format a title and two sub-lines.
Step 1: Type three lines
Open a new Word document and type this exactly, pressing Enter after each line:
MICROSOFT WORD 2007 PRACTICE
Fonts made simple
Learning clean formatting step by step
Step 2: Format the title (line 1)
1. Select line 1
2. Change the font size to **18**
3. Make it **Bold**
4. Change case to **Capitalize Each Word** (so it becomes: Microsoft Word 2007 Practice)

Optional:
- Change font type to something clear like Calibri or Times New Roman

Step 3: Format the two sub-lines (lines 2 and 3)
1. Select line 2
2. Set font size to **14**
3. Make it **Bold**

Then:
1. Select line 3
2. Set font size to **12**
3. Make it Italic (optional)

Step 4: Add one clean color (optional)
If you want to practice color:
- Select line 2 only
- Change font color to dark blue or dark gray Keep the rest black.

Quick check (self-test)
- Where do you find font tools in Word 2007?
- What shortcut makes text bold?
- What is a safe normal font size for body text?
- When should you avoid using many font colors?

CHAPTER 2: PARAGRAPH FORMATTING THAT ACTUALLY MATTERS

Most beginner documents look messy for one reason: paragraph settings are wrong. This chapter teaches the few paragraph tools that make a document look clean immediately.

1) Where Paragraph Tools Are Found
Most paragraph tools are in:
- **Home tab**
- **Paragraph group**

You will use these settings for letters, reports, CVs, and any professional document.

2) Alignment (How Text Sits on the Page)
Alignment controls the left and right edges of your text.

Left Align (most common)
Text lines start at the left edge and have a ragged right edge.
Best for almost all normal writing.
Shortcut: **Ctrl + L**

Center
Text is centered on the page.
Use for titles and short headings.
Shortcut: **Ctrl + E**

Right Align
Text lines end at the right edge.
Use for dates or a short line on the right side.
Shortcut: **Ctrl + R**

Justify
Text touches both left and right edges evenly.
It can look formal, but it may create awkward spacing in some documents.
Shortcut: **Ctrl + J**

Beginner rule:
Use Left Align for body text. Use Center only for titles.

3) Line Spacing (How Much Space Between Lines)
Line spacing affects readability.
Common choices:
- **Single (1.0)**
- **1.15** (often looks clean for everyday work)
- **1.5** (common for school assignments)

- **2.0** (double spacing, common for drafts or teacher requirements)

Beginner rule:

Use one consistent line spacing in a document. Do not mix different line spacings randomly.

4) Spacing Before and After (The Clean Way to Separate Paragraphs)

Spacing Before and After adds space around paragraphs without pressing Enter many times.

This is better than adding blank lines because:
- It stays consistent
- It does not break your page layout
- It prints cleanly

Beginner mistake to avoid:

Do not press Enter repeatedly to create space. Use paragraph spacing instead.

5) Indentation (Where Paragraphs Start)

Indentation moves text in from the margins.

Common types:
- **First-line indent** (the first line moves in a little)
- **Hanging indent** (used for references and bibliographies)
- **Left indent** (moves the entire paragraph right)
- **Right indent** (moves the entire paragraph left from the right side)

Beginner rule:

For letters and reports, do not indent paragraphs randomly. Either use:
- no indent, with spacing between paragraphs, or
- first-line indent consistently

Practice Example: A Neat One-Page Letter (15 to 20 minutes)

Goal: Make a clean letter with correct alignment and spacing.

Step 1: Type this letter exactly

Open a new Word document and type the text below. Press Enter once at the end of each line.

Your Name
Your Address
City, Country
Phone Number
February 3, 2026
The Manager
Company Name
Company Address
City, Country
Subject: Request for Information
Dear Sir/Madam,
I am writing to request more information about your services. I would like to understand your pricing, your working hours, and the steps required to begin.
Please share the details by email or phone at your earliest convenience. Thank you for your time and support.
Sincerely,
Your Name

Step 2: Set clean alignment
1. Select the whole letter (Ctrl + A).
2. Set it to **Left Align** (Ctrl + L).

Step 3: Set line spacing
1. With everything still selected, click **Line Spacing** in the Paragraph group.
2. Choose **1.15** or **1.5** (choose one and keep it consistent).

Step 4: Fix spacing between sections the clean way
Now improve the spacing without pressing Enter many times.
Option A (simple beginner method)
- Keep one blank line between major blocks only:
    o Between address block and date
    o Between date and recipient block
    o Between recipient block and subject
    o Between subject and greeting
    o Between paragraphs
    o Between closing and your name

Option B (better professional method)
1. Select the two body paragraphs only (the "I am writing…" paragraph and the "Please share…" paragraph).

2. Open paragraph settings:
   - Click the small arrow in the bottom-right of the Paragraph group
3. Set:
   - Spacing Before: 0 pt
   - Spacing After: 6 pt or 8 pt
   - Line spacing: keep what you chose (1.15 or 1.5)
4. Click OK.

Step 5: Check the result
Your letter should look clean and balanced:
- No random gaps
- No tight lines
- Clear separation between blocks
- Easy to read

Common beginner problems (quick fixes)
"My letter has strange big gaps."
Cause:
- Extra blank lines, or spacing after paragraphs is too large

Fix:
- Turn on Show/Hide later (you will learn it), or
- Select the letter and reduce Spacing After to 6 pt

"My paragraphs look crowded."
Fix:
- Increase line spacing to 1.15 or 1.5

"My text starts too far from the left margin."
Cause:
- Left indent is set by mistake

Fix:
- Select the paragraph and set Left Indent back to 0

Quick check (self-test)
- Which alignment should most body text use?
- Why is spacing before/after better than pressing Enter many times?
- What line spacing is commonly used for school assignments?
- What is indentation, and why should it be consistent?

CHAPTER 3: BULLETS, NUMBERING, AND MULTILEVEL LISTS

Lists make documents easier to read. But beginners often struggle when numbering "breaks" or when Word changes the list style by itself. This chapter shows you how to create clean lists and fix common list problems.

1) Bullets vs Numbering (When to Use Each)

Bullets (no specific order)
Use bullets when the order does not matter.
Examples:
- shopping list
- list of supplies
- list of ideas

Numbering (steps or rank)
Use numbering when order matters.
Examples:
- instructions
- steps in a process
- priorities (1st, 2nd, 3rd)

Beginner rule:
If it is a step-by-step process, use numbers. If it is just items, use bullets.

2) Where List Tools Are Found
List tools are in:
- **Home tab**
- **Paragraph group**
  Look for:
- **Bullets**
- **Numbering**
- **Multilevel List**

3) Making a Clean Bulleted List
Best practice
1. Type your first item
2. Press **Enter** to go to the next bullet
3. Press **Enter** twice to end the list

Tip:
If Word creates a bullet automatically and you do not want it:
- Press **Backspace** once to remove the bullet, or

- Press **Ctrl + Z** to undo the automatic formatting

4) Making a Clean Numbered List
Best practice
1. Start with step 1
2. Press **Enter** for the next step
3. Press **Enter** twice to end the list

Beginner rule:
Do not type numbers manually (1., 2., 3.) when you can use Word's numbering tool. Word's numbering updates automatically when you insert or delete steps.

5) Restarting Numbering (Most Common Beginner Need)
Sometimes you create a numbered list, then later you want a new list to start from 1 again.

How to restart numbering
1. Click inside the first number where you want the new list to begin
2. Right-click the number
3. Choose **Restart at 1**

If you do not see that option:
- Turn numbering off, press Enter, then turn numbering on again

6) Fixing Broken Lists (Simple Troubleshooting)
Problem A: "My list suddenly becomes 1 again"
Cause:
- You pressed Enter twice and ended the list by accident

Fix:
- Click on the line that should continue the list
- Click **Numbering** again

Problem B: "My numbering becomes weird like 1, a, i"
Cause:
- A multilevel list style was applied

Fix:
- Select the list
- Click the **Numbering** button (not multilevel) to return to normal 1, 2, 3

Problem C: "My bullets or numbers are not aligned"

Cause:
- Indents changed

Fix:
1. Select the list
2. Right-click the list
3. Choose **Adjust List Indents** (or use Paragraph settings)
4. Keep it simple and consistent

7) Multilevel Lists (Simple Explanation)

Multilevel lists are for outlines like:

1
1.1
1.2
2
2.1

They are useful for:
- structured documents
- policies
- outlines

Beginner rule:
Do not use multilevel lists unless you truly need sub-levels. Many beginners turn them on accidentally and get confused.

Practice Example (15 minutes)

Goal: Create a shopping list (bullets) and a 3-step instructions list (numbering).

Step 1: Create a bulleted shopping list

1. Open a new Word document
2. Type this title:
   Shopping List
3. Press Enter
4. Click **Bullets**
5. Type these items, pressing Enter after each one:
   Rice
   Sugar
   Tea
   Cooking oil
   Soap
6. Press Enter twice to end the list

Step 2: Create a 3-step instructions list
1. Type this title:
   How to Save a Document
2. Press Enter
3. Click **Numbering**
4. Type these steps, pressing Enter after each one:
   Click the Office Button
   Choose Save As and select Word Document
   Type a file name and click Save
5. Press Enter twice to end the list

Step 3: Practice restarting numbering
1. Press Enter once
2. Click **Numbering** again
3. Type:
   Open the file later from the Desktop
   If it starts at 4 instead of 1:
- Right-click the number
- Choose **Restart at 1**

Common beginner problems (quick fixes)
"Word keeps continuing my numbering from earlier."
Fix:
- Right-click the number and choose **Restart at 1**

"My list changed shape and became too complex."
Fix:
- Select the list and click **Numbering** (simple) or **Bullets** again

"I cannot stop the list."
Fix:
- Press **Enter** twice

Quick check (self-test)
- When should you use bullets instead of numbering?
- How do you end a list quickly?
- How do you restart numbering at 1?
- What is a multilevel list used for?

CHAPTER 4: STYLES FOR BEGINNERS

Styles are the secret to fast, professional documents. When you use styles, Word keeps your formatting consistent and can automatically build tools like a table of contents later.

1) What a Style Is (Simple Definition)

A style is a ready-made set of formatting that you apply with one click.

Example:

A "Heading 1" style might include:
- a larger font size
- bold text
- spacing before and after
- consistent look across the whole document

Instead of manually changing font and spacing every time, you apply a style once.

2) Why Styles Save Time

Styles keep your document consistent

All headings look the same. All subheadings look the same.

Styles prevent formatting chaos

Beginners often format headings by guessing:
- some headings are size 16
- others are size 14
- spacing is different everywhere

Styles stop that.

Styles help Word understand your document structure

When Word understands your headings, you can:
- create a table of contents automatically
- navigate quickly using headings
- update your table of contents with one click

Beginner rule:

If your document is longer than 2 pages, styles are worth using.

3) Where Styles Are Found

Styles are in:
- **Home tab**
- **Styles group**

Common built-in styles:
- Normal

- Heading 1
- Heading 2
- Heading 3

4) How to Apply Heading Styles (The Right Way)
Heading 1
Use for main sections.
Example:
Introduction
Chapter 1
Conclusion
Heading 2
Use for sub-sections under a main heading.
Example:
Background
Problem statement
Key points
Beginner rule:
Do not skip levels. If you use Heading 2, there should be a Heading 1 above it.

5) Updating Styles (Keeping Headings Consistent)
You might change your mind and want all headings to look different.
Good news:
If you used styles correctly, you can update the style once and Word updates all headings in the document.
Two simple beginner approaches:
Approach A: Change a heading manually, then update the style
1. Click one Heading 1 heading
2. Change its font size or color
3. In the Styles group, right-click **Heading 1**
4. Choose **Update Heading 1 to Match Selection**

Now all Heading 1 headings change to match.
Approach B: Modify the style directly
1. Right-click **Heading 1**
2. Click **Modify**
3. Choose font, size, spacing
4. Click OK

Beginner rule:
Only update styles after you have tested the look on one heading first.

Practice Example (15 minutes)
Goal: Apply Heading 1 and Heading 2 to a short report.
Step 1: Type this short report
Open a new Word document and type the following exactly. Press Enter where you see blank lines.
Mobile Data Challenges in My Area
Introduction
Mobile data is expensive and sometimes unstable. This affects study, work, and communication.
Common Problems
Slow speed during peak hours
High data costs
Weak signal in some areas
Possible Solutions
Use data at off-peak times
Download videos at night for later viewing
Use Wi-Fi where available
Conclusion
Better access to affordable and stable internet improves learning and productivity.
Step 2: Apply Heading 1 to the main title
1. Select: Mobile Data Challenges in My Area
2. Click **Heading 1** in the Styles group

Step 3: Apply Heading 2 to section headings
For each of these lines, select the heading and click **Heading 2**:
- Introduction
- Common Problems
- Possible Solutions
- Conclusion

Leave the paragraphs under each heading as Normal text.

Step 4: Update Heading 2 style (optional practice)
Goal: Make all Heading 2 headings slightly larger.
1. Click on one Heading 2 heading (example: Introduction)

2. Increase its font size by 1 or 2 points
3. Right-click **Heading 2** in the Styles group
4. Click **Update Heading 2 to Match Selection**

Now all Heading 2 headings should change.

Common beginner problems (quick fixes)
"My headings changed, but only one of them changed."
Cause:
You formatted it manually instead of using styles.
Fix:
Apply Heading 1 or Heading 2 from the Styles group to all headings.
"My headings look too big or ugly."
Fix:
Modify the style once (Heading 1 or Heading 2). Do not fix each heading one by one.
"My headings are not in the Styles box."
Fix:
Make sure you are on the Home tab and looking in the Styles group.

Quick check (self-test)
- What is a style?
- Why are styles better than manual formatting?
- What should Heading 1 be used for?
- How do you update a style so all headings change?

CHAPTER 5: FORMAT PAINTER AND CLEARING FORMATTING

This chapter gives you two "cleanup" tools that every beginner needs:
- Format Painter (copy formatting)
- Clear Formatting (remove messy formatting)

If you learn these, you will fix messy documents much faster.

1) Format Painter (Copy Formatting)
What Format Painter does

Format Painter copies formatting from one place and applies it somewhere else.

It copies things like:
- font type and size
- bold/italic/underline
- font color
- paragraph alignment
- spacing

It does not copy the words, only the look.

Where to find it
- **Home tab**
- **Clipboard group**
- **Format Painter** (paintbrush icon)

How to use Format Painter (one-time use)
1. Select the text that has the formatting you want
2. Click **Format Painter**
3. Select the text you want to format
   Formatting will be applied, then Format Painter turns off.

How to use Format Painter (multiple uses)
1. Select the text with the correct formatting
2. Double-click **Format Painter**
3. Click or drag across multiple places to apply the same formatting
4. Press **Esc** to turn it off

Beginner tip:

Format Painter is best when you have one heading that looks perfect and you want other headings to match it quickly.

2) Clear Formatting (Reset Messy Text)
What Clear Formatting does

Clear Formatting removes most direct formatting and returns text to a clean default look.

It is useful when:
- you pasted text from the internet
- fonts and sizes are mixed
- spacing looks strange
- text looks bold or colored by mistake

Where to find it
- **Home tab**
- **Font group**
- **Clear Formatting** (often looks like an eraser or an "A" with an eraser)

Beginner rule:
If your paragraph looks messy and you do not know why, Clear Formatting is often the fastest fix.

3) The Safe Cleanup Method (Best Order)

When text looks messy, do this order:
1. Select the messy text
2. Click **Clear Formatting**
3. Reapply the correct style or formatting (Normal, Heading, etc.)
4. Use Format Painter if you want to match another clean section

Practice Example (15 minutes)

Goal: Clean a messy paragraph using Clear Formatting.

Step 1: Create a "messy paragraph"

Open a new Word document and type this paragraph:
I want my document to look clean and professional. Mixed fonts and strange spacing make it hard to read.

Now deliberately make it messy:
1. Select the words "look clean" and make them bold
2. Select "professional" and change its font size to 18
3. Select "Mixed fonts" and change its font color to red
4. Select "hard to read" and underline it

Your paragraph should now look inconsistent.

Step 2: Clear the formatting
1. Select the whole paragraph
2. Click **Clear Formatting**

Expected result:
The paragraph returns to a plain, consistent look.
Step 3: Make it clean again
Now format it properly:
1. Set the whole paragraph to a normal font size (11 or 12)
2. Make only one phrase bold, if needed (example: "clean and professional")

Keep it simple.

Bonus practice (Format Painter)
Goal: Make one heading match another.
1. Type two headings:
   Heading One
   Heading Two
2. Format "Heading One" to look like a heading (bigger and bold).
3. Copy that look to "Heading Two":
- Select "Heading One"
- Click **Format Painter**
- Select "Heading Two"

Common beginner problems (quick fixes)
"Clear Formatting removed too much."
Fix:
- Press **Ctrl + Z** (Undo), then clear smaller parts, or apply a style after clearing.

"Format Painter changed my spacing too."
Reason:
Format Painter copies paragraph formatting too.
Fix:
- Use it on smaller selections (just the heading text), or
- Apply styles instead of manual formatting when possible.

"My document still looks messy after clearing."
Fix:
- Clear formatting, then apply a Style (Normal, Heading 1, Heading 2). Styles rebuild consistency.

Quick check (self-test)

- What does Format Painter copy?
- What does Clear Formatting remove?
- When should you use Clear Formatting first?
- What key turns off Format Painter when it is locked on?

PART IV: PAGE SETUP AND DOCUMENT LAYOUT
CHAPTER 1: PAGE SETUP BASICS

Page setup controls how your document sits on paper. If your margins are wrong or your paper size is incorrect, your document can print badly even if the text looks fine on the screen.

This chapter covers:
- margins
- page orientation
- paper size

1) Where Page Setup Tools Are Found

Most page setup tools are in:
- **Page Layout tab**
- **Page Setup group**

2) Margins (The Empty Space Around Your Text)

Margins are the blank spaces at the top, bottom, left, and right of the page.

Why margins matter:
- They make the page readable
- They leave space for binding or stapling
- They prevent text from being cut off when printed

Common margin choices:
- **Normal** (good default)
- **Narrow** (fits more text, but can look crowded)
- **Wide** (more space, looks formal)

Beginner rule:

For school assignments, use Normal margins unless your school gives specific rules.

How to set margins
1. Click the **Page Layout** tab
2. Click **Margins**
3. Choose **Normal**

If you need custom margins
1. Page Layout tab
2. Click **Margins**
3. Click **Custom Margins**
4. Type your values
5. Click **OK**

3) Orientation (Portrait vs Landscape)
Orientation controls whether the page is vertical or horizontal.
Portrait
Most common. Good for letters, reports, school assignments.
Landscape
Wide page. Good for tables, charts, and wide layouts.
Beginner rule:
Use Portrait for normal documents. Switch to Landscape only when the content is too wide.
How to change orientation
1. Page Layout tab
2. Click **Orientation**
3. Choose **Portrait** or **Landscape**

4) Paper Size (Match the Paper You Will Print On)
Paper size controls the size of the page in Word.
Common paper sizes:
- **Letter** (common in the United States)
- **A4** (common in many other countries)

Beginner warning:
If your Word paper size does not match the real paper in the printer, printing can look wrong.
How to set paper size
1. Page Layout tab
2. Click **Size**
3. Choose **Letter** or **A4** (based on what you will print on)

Practice Example (10 to 15 minutes)
Goal: Set margins for a school assignment.
Step 1: Create a new document
Open Word 2007 and start a blank document.
Step 2: Set the paper size (choose one)
If you are printing in the United States, choose:
- **Letter**

If you are printing in many other regions, choose:
- **A4**

How:
1. Page Layout tab

2. Size
   3. Choose Letter or A4

Step 3: Set margins
   1. Page Layout tab
   2. Margins
   3. Choose **Normal**

If your assignment requires custom margins, example:
- Left: 1.5 inches (for binding)
- Top, Right, Bottom: 1 inch

How:
   1. Page Layout tab
   2. Margins
   3. Custom Margins
   4. Enter the values
   5. OK

Step 4: Confirm orientation
   1. Page Layout tab
   2. Orientation
   3. Choose **Portrait**

Step 5: Type a test heading and paragraph

Type:

School Assignment Practice

Then type one short paragraph below it.

This helps you see how the margins look on the page.

Common beginner problems (quick fixes)

"My text is too close to the edge."

Fix:
- Increase margins using Page Layout > Margins > Normal or Custom Margins

"My printed page cuts off lines."

Fix:
- Confirm paper size matches the printer paper (Letter vs A4)

"My page looks sideways."

Fix:
- Set Orientation back to Portrait

Quick check (self-test)
- What do margins control?

- When should you use Landscape orientation?
- Why must paper size match the real paper?
- Where do you change margins in Word 2007?

CHAPTER 2: PAGE BREAKS AND SECTION BREAKS

Beginners often create new pages by pressing Enter many times. That works for a moment, but it breaks later when you add or delete text. Page breaks and section breaks are the clean, professional way to control pages.

This chapter explains:
- what a page break is
- what a section break is
- when to use each
- the most common beginner mistakes

1) Page Break (Start a New Page Cleanly)

What a page break does

A page break forces the next text to start at the top of the next page.

When to use a page break

Use a page break when you want a new page but the page layout stays the same.

Examples:
- title page, then Chapter 1 starts on the next page
- ending one section of an assignment and starting another on a new page
- starting a new letter page if the letter is long

How to insert a page break

Method A (fast keyboard method)
- Press **Ctrl + Enter**

Method B (from the Ribbon)
1. Click the **Insert** tab
2. Click **Page Break**

Beginner rule:
Use Ctrl + Enter instead of pressing Enter many times.

2) Section Break (Change Layout Inside the Same Document)

What a section break does

A section break lets you change page settings in one part of the document without affecting the rest.

Examples of what section breaks allow:
- different headers and footers in different parts
- changing page numbering style (i, ii, 1, 2)

- switching one part to landscape (for a wide table), then back to portrait
- different margins in different sections

Types of section breaks (beginner level)
- Next Page: starts a new section on the next page (most common)
- Continuous: starts a new section on the same page (more advanced)

Where to insert a section break (Word 2007)
1. Click the **Page Layout** tab
2. Click **Breaks**
3. Under Section Breaks, choose **Next Page** (most common)

Beginner rule:
If you are not changing layout, use a page break.
If you need different headers, numbering, orientation, or margins, use a section break.

3) Common Beginner Errors (And Fixes)

Error 1: Pressing Enter many times to make a new page
Problem:
When you edit earlier text, your "new page" moves and becomes messy.
Fix:
Delete extra blank lines and insert a real page break (Ctrl + Enter).

Error 2: Using a section break when you only needed a page break
Problem:
Your headers, footers, and numbering can behave strangely.
Fix:
Remove the section break and use a page break instead.

Error 3: Not knowing why page numbers restart or change
Cause:
A section break was inserted.
Fix:
Check for section breaks and remove or manage them properly.

4) How to See Breaks (So You Can Fix Them)
Word can show hidden formatting marks, including breaks.
How:
- Home tab
- Paragraph group
- Click **Show/Hide** (the ¶ symbol)

This helps you see:
- Page Break
- Section Break (Next Page)
- extra paragraph marks

Beginner tip:
If your document is behaving strangely, turn this on.

Practice Example (15 minutes)
Goal: Create a title page, then start page 2 correctly.
Step 1: Create a new document
Open Word 2007 and start a blank document.
Step 2: Create a simple title page
Type this (centered is fine):
Microsoft Word 2007 Practice
A Beginner Report
Your Name
February 3, 2026
Tip:
You can center this page:
- Select the lines
- Press **Ctrl + E**

Step 3: Start page 2 correctly
Do not press Enter many times.
Use a page break:
- Press **Ctrl + Enter**

Now you are on page 2 at the top.
Step 4: Type the start of your report on page 2
Type:
Introduction
This report is a practice document to learn clean page setup in Microsoft Word 2007.
Step 5: Confirm it worked
Look at the Status Bar:
- It should show you are on **Page 2**

Optional check:
- Turn on Show/Hide (¶) to see the page break line.

Quick check (self-test)
- What does a page break do?
- What does a section break do that a page break cannot do?
- What shortcut inserts a page break?
- Why should you avoid pressing Enter many times to create a new page?

CHAPTER 3: HEADERS, FOOTERS, AND PAGE NUMBERS

Headers and footers are areas at the top and bottom of each page. They are used for repeated information such as your name, document title, date, and page numbers.

This chapter covers:
- headers
- footers
- page numbers
- different first page option
- simple page number formats

1) What Headers and Footers Are

Header

The header is the space at the top of the page. It prints on every page by default.

Common header uses:
- your name
- document title
- class name or course code
- organization name

Footer

The footer is the space at the bottom of the page. It prints on every page by default.

Common footer uses:
- page numbers
- date
- short notes (rare)

Beginner rule:
Keep headers and footers simple. Too much text looks crowded.

2) How to Open the Header and Footer Area

Method A (fast mouse method)
- Double-click near the top of the page to open the header
- Double-click near the bottom of the page to open the footer

Method B (from the Ribbon)
1. Click the **Insert** tab
2. Click **Header** or **Footer**

3. Choose a simple built-in style (or choose Edit Header / Edit Footer)

3) Adding Page Numbers (Simple and Clean)
How to add page numbers at the bottom
1. Click the **Insert** tab
2. Click **Page Number**
3. Point to **Bottom of Page**
4. Choose a simple style (example: Plain Number)

Word places page numbers in the footer automatically.

4) Page Number Formats (Common Beginner Needs)
Sometimes you need to change how page numbers look.
Examples:
- 1, 2, 3
- Page 1 of 5
- i, ii, iii (usually for front pages)

How to change number format
1. Insert tab
2. Page Number
3. Click **Format Page Numbers**
4. Choose:
    - Number format (1, 2, 3 or i, ii, iii)
    - Start at (usually 1)
5. Click OK

Beginner rule:
For most documents, keep 1, 2, 3 and start at 1.

5) Different First Page (Very Useful for Assignments)
Sometimes you want:
- no header and footer on the title page
- but page numbers starting from page 2

Word can do this with one setting.

How to make the first page different
1. Open the header or footer area (double-click top or bottom)
2. In the Header and Footer Tools (Design tab that appears), check:
    - **Different First Page**

Now the first page header/footer becomes separate from the rest.

Beginner note:

This does not automatically remove the first page content. It just lets you format it differently.

Practice Example (15 to 20 minutes)

Goal: Add "Your Name" in the header and page numbers at the bottom.

Step 1: Create a 2-page document
1. Open a new document
2. Type a short title:
   Header and Footer Practice
3. Press Enter a few times and type a short paragraph (any text)
4. Insert a page break:
   - Press **Ctrl + Enter**
5. Type another paragraph on page 2

You now have at least 2 pages.

Step 2: Add "Your Name" in the header
1. Double-click at the top of page 1
2. The header area opens
3. Type:
   Your Name

Tip:

If you want it on the right side:
- Press **Ctrl + R**

Step 3: Add page numbers at the bottom
1. Click outside the header to return to the document, or keep the header open
2. Click the **Insert** tab
3. Click **Page Number**
4. Bottom of Page
5. Choose a simple style

Step 4: Close header and footer
- Click **Close Header and Footer** on the Ribbon, or
- Double-click in the main document area

Optional practice: Different first page (title page)

Goal: No header on page 1, but keep header on page 2.

1. Double-click the header area
2. Check **Different First Page**
3. Click into the header on page 1 and delete "Your Name" (if it appears there)
4. Scroll to page 2 and confirm the header still shows "Your Name"

Result:
- Page 1 can be blank in header
- Page 2 and onward keep the header

Common beginner problems (quick fixes)
"I typed my name, but it shows on every page."
That is normal for a header.
Fix:
If you want the first page different, enable **Different First Page**.

"I cannot exit the header."
Fix:
- Click **Close Header and Footer**, or
- Double-click the main document area.

"My page numbers disappeared."
Cause:
You may have deleted the footer content.
Fix:
Insert them again using Insert > Page Number.

Quick check (self-test)
- What is a header used for?
- What is a footer commonly used for?
- How do you insert page numbers at the bottom?
- What does Different First Page do?

CHAPTER 4: COLUMNS AND PAGE BACKGROUND TOOLS

This chapter introduces four layout tools that change how a page looks:
- columns
- page borders
- watermark
- page color

These tools are useful for newsletters, flyers, notices, and drafts.

1) Columns (Split Text Into Two or More Vertical Sections)

Columns divide a page into vertical blocks, like a newspaper.

When to use columns
- newsletters
- church announcements
- short brochures
- long lists that fit better in two columns

Beginner rule:
Use columns only when the document is meant to look like a newsletter. Do not use columns for normal school essays.

How to apply columns
1. Click the **Page Layout** tab
2. Click **Columns**
3. Choose **Two** (or another option)

Tip:
If you want columns for only one part of a document, you usually need section breaks. As a beginner, practice with a full page first.

2) Page Borders (A Border Around the Page)

A page border draws a line or design around the edge of the page.

When page borders are useful
- certificates
- formal announcements
- invitations
- official letters (rare, depending on style)

Beginner warning:
Page borders can look unprofessional if overused. Use simple borders.

How to add a page border
1. Click the **Page Layout** tab
2. Click **Page Borders**
3. Choose a simple **Box** border
4. Choose line style and width
5. Click **OK**

3) Watermark (A Faint Word Behind Your Text)
A watermark is light text behind the main text, like:
- DRAFT
- CONFIDENTIAL
- SAMPLE

When watermarks are useful
- draft documents
- training materials
- internal office documents

How to add a watermark
1. Click the **Page Layout** tab
2. Click **Watermark**
3. Choose a built-in option (like DRAFT) or choose **Custom Watermark** for your own text

Beginner rule:
Use watermarks only when you have a clear reason.

4) Page Color (Background Color of the Page)
Page color changes the page background.

When page color is useful
- flyers and notices
- on-screen reading materials
- creative documents

Beginner warning:
Most printers do not print page color well unless you choose special settings. Page color can also waste ink.

How to change page color
1. Click the **Page Layout** tab
2. Click **Page Color**
3. Choose a color, or choose **No Color** to remove it

Beginner rule:
Avoid page color for normal printed reports.

Practice Example (20 minutes)
Goal: Make a simple 2-column newsletter page.
Step 1: Create a new document
Open Word 2007 and start a blank document.
Step 2: Add a title
1. Type this title on the first line:
   Community Newsletter
2. Center it:
- Select the title
- Press **Ctrl + E**
3. Make it bold and larger (example: 18)

Step 3: Start your newsletter text
Press Enter once and type this text (you can copy it exactly):
This newsletter shares short updates, announcements, and helpful information for our community. It is written in a simple format that is easy to read.
Announcements
1. Meeting on Saturday at 10:00 AM.
2. Clean-up activity on Sunday at 4:00 PM.
3. Training session next week for new volunteers.

Short Note
Good communication builds trust. Please share updates early so they can be included in the next issue.

Step 4: Apply two columns
1. Click anywhere in the body text (below the title)
2. Click **Page Layout**
3. Click **Columns**
4. Choose **Two**

What you should see:
Your body text flows into two columns.
Tip:
If the title also becomes two columns and you want the title to stay full width, do this beginner-friendly fix:
- Put the cursor after the title line
- Insert a page break and practice again
  Better method (later in the book): section breaks.

Step 5: Add a simple page border (optional)

1. Page Layout tab
2. Page Borders
3. Choose Box
4. Choose a thin line
5. OK

Step 6: Add a watermark (optional)
1. Page Layout tab
2. Watermark
3. Choose DRAFT

Step 7: Remove background color (keep clean)
If you added page color by mistake:
- Page Layout > Page Color > No Color

Common beginner problems (quick fixes)
"My text jumps strangely between columns."
Cause:
- Extra paragraph marks or manual spaces.

Fix:
- Delete extra blank lines, then let Word flow text naturally.

"My title is also in columns."
Fix:
- For now, accept it for practice.
- Later you will learn how to keep the title full width using section breaks.

"My printed page border is cut off."
Cause:
- Printer margins differ.

Fix:
- Use a simpler border or increase margins.

Quick check (self-test)
- What are columns used for?
- Where do you find Columns in Word 2007?
- When is a watermark helpful?
- Why should you be careful with page color when printing?

PART V: INSERT TOOLS YOU WILL USE OFTEN (INSERT TAB)
CHAPTER 1: PICTURES DONE RIGHT

Pictures can improve a document, but beginners often struggle with one problem: the picture "moves" or text jumps around. The key is learning how to insert pictures and control text wrapping.

This chapter covers:
- insert a picture
- resize it correctly
- crop it
- wrap text around it
- position it neatly

1) Insert a Picture
Where to insert pictures
1. Click the **Insert** tab
2. Click **Picture**
3. Choose the image file from your computer
4. Click **Insert**

Beginner rule:
Insert the picture first, then adjust it. Do not try to format before it is in the document.

2) Resize a Picture (Without Stretching It)
The right way to resize
- Click the picture once (handles appear around it)
- Drag a corner handle inward or outward

Why corners matter:
Corner resizing keeps the picture shape correct.

Beginner warning:
Do not drag the side handles unless you want to stretch the image. Stretching makes pictures look unprofessional.

Tip:
If the picture becomes too large:
- Use Undo (Ctrl + Z)
- Then resize from a corner again

3) Crop a Picture (Remove Unwanted Parts)
Cropping removes the parts you do not want.
How to crop in Word 2007

1. Click the picture
2. A new tab appears: **Picture Tools > Format**
3. Click **Crop**
4. Drag the crop handles to keep only the part you want
5. Click **Crop** again (or click outside the image) to finish

Beginner tip:
Crop first, then resize. It is easier to control the final look.

4) Text Wrapping (The Most Important Picture Skill)

Text wrapping controls how text behaves around a picture. Common options:
- In Line with Text
- Square
- Tight
- Top and Bottom
- Behind Text
- In Front of Text

Beginner rule:
For most documents, "Square" is the easiest and cleanest.

How to set text wrapping
1. Click the picture
2. Go to **Picture Tools > Format**
3. Click **Text Wrapping**
4. Choose **Square**

Or:
- Right-click the picture
- Choose **Text Wrapping**
- Choose **Square**

5) Positioning a Picture (Make It Look Neat)

Once wrapping is set to Square:
- Click and drag the picture to where you want it
- The text will flow around it

Simple placement tips:
- Keep pictures near the paragraph that talks about them
- Avoid placing pictures too close to the page edges
- Keep consistent size if you use multiple pictures in one document

Beginner warning:
Avoid "Behind Text" until you are confident. It can make text hard to read and difficult to edit.

Practice Example (15 minutes)
Goal: Insert a photo and wrap text "Square".
Step 1: Create a short practice page
Open a new Word document and type this paragraph:
Pictures can help explain ideas and make a document more engaging. When I insert a picture correctly and use Square text wrapping, the text stays clean and the picture is easy to place.
Press Enter once.
Step 2: Insert a picture
1. Click the **Insert** tab
2. Click **Picture**
3. Choose any photo on your computer
4. Click **Insert**

Step 3: Resize it correctly
1. Click the picture
2. Drag a corner handle to make it medium size (not too large)

Step 4: Set text wrapping to Square
1. Click the picture
2. Click **Picture Tools > Format**
3. Click **Text Wrapping**
4. Choose **Square**

Step 5: Position the picture
1. Click and drag the picture to the right side of the paragraph
2. Watch the text wrap around it

Expected result:
- The picture sits beside the text
- The paragraph wraps cleanly around the picture

Optional:
- Crop the picture if it includes too much background

Common beginner problems (quick fixes)
"I cannot move the picture freely."
Cause:
The picture is set to "In Line with Text".

Fix:
Set wrapping to **Square**.
"The text looks messy and jumps strangely."
Fix:
- Use Square wrapping
- Avoid too many blank lines
- Keep picture size reasonable

"My picture looks stretched."
Fix:
Undo, then resize using corner handles only.

Quick check (self-test)
- Where do you insert a picture from?
- Why should you resize from the corners?
- Which wrapping option is best for beginners most of the time?
- Where do you find Crop in Word 2007?

CHAPTER 2: SHAPES, TEXT BOXES, AND WORDART

Shapes, text boxes, and WordArt help you create simple designs inside Word 2007. Beginners often use them for callouts, quotes, announcements, and small flyers.

This chapter covers:
- inserting shapes
- inserting text boxes
- simple alignment
- grouping objects
- WordArt basics
- a boxed quote practice task

1) Shapes (Simple Visual Elements)

Shapes include:
- rectangles and squares
- arrows
- circles and ovals
- callouts (speech bubbles)

Where to insert shapes
1. Click the **Insert** tab
2. Click **Shapes**
3. Choose a shape
4. Click and drag on the page to draw it

Editing a shape

After you insert a shape:
- click it to select it
- drag corner handles to resize
- drag to move it

Shape formatting appears under a contextual tab:
- **Drawing Tools > Format**

2) Text Boxes (Text Inside a Movable Box)

A text box is a container for text that you can move around the page.

Use text boxes for:
- quotes
- side notes
- announcements
- contact details

- highlight messages

Where to insert a text box
1. Click the **Insert** tab
2. Click **Text Box**
3. Choose a built-in text box, or choose **Draw Text Box**
4. Click and drag to draw the box
5. Type inside it

Beginner rule:
Text boxes are easiest to control when text wrapping is not "In Line with Text." If moving feels hard, change wrapping later using the Format tab.

3) WordArt (Decorative Text)

WordArt creates stylized text, mainly for flyers and simple titles.

Beginner warning:
WordArt can look unprofessional in formal letters and reports. Use it only for posters or announcements.

Where to insert WordArt
1. Click the **Insert** tab
2. Click **WordArt**
3. Choose a style
4. Type your text
5. Click OK

4) Alignment (Make Objects Look Neat)

When you place shapes or text boxes, alignment makes them look professional.

Simple alignment methods:
- Use the mouse to line things up carefully
- Use built-in Align tools (best)

Where Align tools are found
1. Click the object (shape or text box)
2. Go to **Drawing Tools > Format**
3. Find **Align** (or related Arrange tools)

Common align choices:
- Align Left
- Align Center
- Align Right
- Align Top

- Align Middle
- Align Bottom

Beginner rule:
If your flyer looks messy, it is usually an alignment problem.

5) Grouping (Keep Items Together)

Grouping locks multiple objects together so they move as one unit.

Use grouping when:
- a text box sits on top of a shape
- you want to move them together
- you do not want the layout to break

How to group objects
1. Hold **Ctrl** and click each object you want to group
2. Right-click one selected object
3. Click **Group > Group**

To ungroup:
- Right-click the grouped object
- Group > Ungroup

Beginner tip:
Grouping works best when objects are not "In Line with Text."

Practice Example (15 to 20 minutes)

Goal: Create a boxed quote using a text box.

Step 1: Type a short paragraph
Open a new document and type this paragraph:
This document includes a short quote in a box to draw attention. Text boxes are useful for highlighting important messages.
Press Enter twice.

Step 2: Insert a text box
1. Click the **Insert** tab
2. Click **Text Box**
3. Choose **Draw Text Box**
4. Click and drag to draw a medium box under your paragraph

Step 3: Type the quote inside the text box
Type this inside the box:
"Good formatting makes your writing easier to read."

Step 4: Format the box to look clean
1. Click the border of the text box (not inside the text)
2. Go to **Drawing Tools > Format**

Make these simple changes:
- Shape Fill: light gray or no fill
- Shape Outline: black or dark gray
- Line weight: thin or medium

Step 5: Center the quote (optional)
1. Click inside the quote text
2. Press **Ctrl + E** to center it

Step 6: Move the text box neatly
Click the border and drag it slightly so it sits cleanly under your paragraph.
Optional:
Resize from corners so it is not too wide.

Common beginner problems (quick fixes)
"I cannot select the text box border."
Fix:
- Click the edge of the box, not inside the text.

"The text box moves strangely and breaks my layout."
Fix:
- Change text wrapping of the text box to Square:
    o Click the text box border
    o Drawing Tools > Format
    o Text Wrapping (or Arrange) > choose Square

"Grouping is not working."
Cause:
One object might be In Line with Text.
Fix:
Change wrapping to Square for both objects, then group again.

Quick check (self-test)
- Where do you insert a text box?
- What is the difference between WordArt and normal text?
- Why do people group objects?
- Which tool helps you line objects up neatly?

CHAPTER 3: TABLES FOR BEGINNERS

Tables help you organize information into rows and columns. Beginners use tables for timetables, lists, price tables, simple forms, and schedules.

This chapter covers:
- creating a table
- adding rows and columns
- merging cells
- borders and shading
- a simple 3-column timetable practice task

1) What a Table Is
A table is a grid made of:
- columns (vertical)
- rows (horizontal)
- cells (the boxes where you type)

Beginner rule:
A table is not only for numbers. It is also a clean way to align text neatly.

2) Create a Table
Method A: Insert table using the grid (fastest)
1. Click the **Insert** tab
2. Click **Table**
3. Move your mouse over the grid to select the size
4. Click to insert

Example:
To create 3 columns and 5 rows, highlight 3 x 5 on the grid and click.

Method B: Insert table by typing the numbers
1. Insert tab
2. Table
3. Insert Table
4. Choose:
    - Number of columns
    - Number of rows
5. Click OK

3) Adding Rows and Columns
Add a row

Method A:
- Click inside the last cell of the last row
- Press **Tab**
  Word adds a new row automatically.

Method B:
1. Click inside the table
2. A contextual tab appears: **Table Tools**
3. Click **Layout**
4. Use:
   - Insert Above
   - Insert Below

Add a column
1. Click inside the table
2. Table Tools > Layout
3. Use:
   - Insert Left
   - Insert Right

Beginner tip:
If your table feels "stuck," click inside it once to make Table Tools appear.

4) Merge Cells (Combine Boxes)

Merging cells combines two or more cells into one.
Use merging for:
- a table title row
- headings that span across multiple columns

How to merge cells
1. Select the cells you want to merge
2. Table Tools > Layout
3. Click **Merge Cells**

To split a merged cell:
- Table Tools > Layout > Split Cells

5) Borders and Shading (Make the Table Look Clean)
Borders
Borders are the lines around table cells.
To change borders:
1. Click inside the table
2. Table Tools > Design
3. Choose border style and line thickness

4. Use Borders options (All Borders, Outside Borders, etc.)

Shading

Shading adds background color to cells.
Use shading to:
- highlight headers
- make the table easier to scan

How:
1. Select cells
2. Table Tools > Design
3. Click **Shading** and choose a light color

Beginner rule:
Use light shading for headings only. Too many colors make tables hard to read.

Practice Example (20 minutes)

Goal: Make a simple 3-column timetable.

Step 1: Insert a 3-column table
1. Open a new Word document
2. Insert tab > Table
3. Select **3 columns** and **6 rows**
4. Click to insert

Step 2: Create column headings

In the first row, type:
Column 1: Time
Column 2: Activity
Column 3: Notes

Make the headings bold:
- select the first row
- press **Ctrl + B**

Optional:
Shade the first row light gray:
- select the first row
- Table Tools > Design > Shading > light gray

Step 3: Fill the timetable rows

Type example entries like these (one row per entry):
8:00 AM | Study | Focus on typing practice
10:00 AM | Break | Short walk
11:00 AM | Word practice | Formatting and spacing

2:00 PM | Writing | Draft one page
4:00 PM | Review | Fix errors and save files

You can create your own schedule. The goal is to practice table structure.

Step 4: Adjust column width (simple method)

Move your mouse to the vertical line between columns.
When you see the double-arrow cursor, drag to resize.
Suggested beginner layout:
- Time column narrower
- Activity column medium
- Notes column wider

Step 5: Merge a title row (optional)

Make a title above the timetable inside the table.
1. Insert a new row above the header row:
   - Click in the first row
   - Table Tools > Layout > Insert Above
2. Select the three cells in the new top row
3. Click Merge Cells
4. Type:
   Daily Timetable
5. Center it and bold it:
- Ctrl + E
- Ctrl + B

Common beginner problems (quick fixes)

"My text does not align neatly in the cells."
Fix:
- Click in a cell and use normal paragraph alignment (Left Align is fine)

"My table lines look too heavy or too light."
Fix:
- Table Tools > Design
- Choose a different border weight, then apply All Borders

"I cannot see Table Tools."
Fix:
- Click inside the table once. The Table Tools tabs appear only when the table is selected.

Quick check (self-test)

- Where do you insert a table from?
- How do you add a new row quickly using the keyboard?
- What does Merge Cells do?
- Why is shading useful for headings?

CHAPTER 4: SMARTART AND CHARTS

SmartArt and Charts help you present information visually. Beginners should use them only when a visual makes the message clearer than plain text.

This chapter covers:
- when SmartArt is useful
- when Charts are useful
- basic editing for both
- a practice task: a 4-step process SmartArt

1) SmartArt (Visual Diagrams)
What SmartArt is

SmartArt is a tool that turns words into simple diagrams. Common SmartArt types:
- Process (steps in order)
- List (grouped ideas)
- Cycle (repeating loop)
- Hierarchy (organization chart)
- Relationship (connections)

When to use SmartArt

Use SmartArt when you want to show:
- steps in a process
- the structure of something (levels)
- a simple flow of ideas
- a quick summary for readers

When not to use SmartArt

Avoid SmartArt when:
- a normal numbered list is clearer
- you have too much text
- your document is formal and the diagram adds no value

Beginner rule:
If your SmartArt needs long sentences, do not use SmartArt. Use a normal list instead.

2) Charts (Visual Data)
What a chart is

A chart displays numbers visually, such as:
- bar chart

- column chart
- pie chart
- line chart

Charts are best when you have real numeric data.

When to use charts

Use charts when you want to show:
- comparisons (this vs that)
- change over time (months, years)
- proportions (how a whole is divided)

When not to use charts

Avoid charts when:
- you do not have numbers
- you only have opinions or descriptions
- the chart would confuse more than it helps

Beginner rule:
No numbers, no chart.

3) How to Insert SmartArt (Basic Steps)

1. Click the **Insert** tab
2. Click **SmartArt**
3. Choose a category (Process is common)
4. Choose a design
5. Click OK
6. Type your text into the SmartArt text pane (or click inside the shapes)

4) How to Edit SmartArt (Beginner Level)

When you click SmartArt, Word shows:
- **SmartArt Tools** (Design and Format tabs)

Common beginner edits:
- Change Colors
- Change SmartArt Style
- Add Shape (add another step)
- Promote/Demote (move levels)

Beginner tip:
Use the text pane. It is usually the easiest way to enter and edit text.

5) How to Insert a Chart (Basic Steps)

1. Click **Insert** tab

2. Click **Chart**
3. Choose a chart type (Column is easiest)
4. Click OK
5. Word opens a small spreadsheet window where you type your data
6. Close the spreadsheet window and the chart updates in Word

Beginner warning:
If your chart looks wrong, the problem is usually the data table, not the chart.

Practice Example (15 to 20 minutes)
Goal: Create a simple process SmartArt with 4 steps.
Step 1: Insert a Process SmartArt
1. Open a new Word document
2. Click **Insert**
3. Click **SmartArt**
4. Click **Process**
5. Choose a simple design such as "Basic Process"
6. Click OK

Step 2: Enter four steps
If the text pane appears on the left, type:
Plan
Write
Edit
Save
If you do not see the text pane:
- Click the small arrow on the left edge of the SmartArt to open it, or
- Click inside each shape and type directly

Step 3: Make the SmartArt easy to read
1. Click the SmartArt once
2. Go to **SmartArt Tools > Design**
3. Choose **Change Colors** and select a simple color set
4. Optional: choose a SmartArt Style that is clean (avoid heavy 3D)

Step 4: Resize and position it neatly
- Click the SmartArt border
- Drag corner handles to resize
- Center it on the page if you want:

- o select it
- o press **Ctrl + E** (only if it is behaving like an object that can be centered)

Common beginner problems (quick fixes)
"My SmartArt has too many shapes."
Fix:
- Click the SmartArt
- SmartArt Tools > Design
- Remove extra text lines in the text pane, or delete a shape

"My text is too long and does not fit."
Fix:
- Shorten words, or use a numbered list instead

"My chart or SmartArt moves oddly."
Fix:
- Set text wrapping to Square:
  - o click the object
  - o Format tab > Text Wrapping > Square

Quick check (self-test)
- When is SmartArt better than a normal list?
- When should you avoid SmartArt?
- What kind of information should a chart display?
- Where do you type data when creating a chart?

CHAPTER 5: SYMBOLS AND EQUATIONS (BASIC USE)

Symbols and equations help you type characters that are not on your keyboard. Beginners often need them for school work, simple math, science, business notes, and copyright marks.
This chapter covers:
- inserting symbols
- common academic symbols
- basic equation use
- a short practice task

1) Symbols (Special Characters)
What symbols are
Symbols include things like:
- $\pm$ (plus/minus)
- © (copyright)
- ® (registered)
- ™ (trademark)
- $\neq$ (not equal)
- $\leq$ (less than or equal to)
- $\geq$ (greater than or equal to)

2) How to Insert a Symbol
1. Click the **Insert** tab
2. Click **Symbol**
3. Choose a symbol from the list, or click **More Symbols**
4. Select the symbol
5. Click **Insert**
6. Click **Close**

Beginner tip:
When you insert a symbol once, Word often remembers it and shows it in the short Symbol list next time.

3) Choosing the Right Font for Symbols
Some symbols appear only in certain fonts.
If you cannot find a symbol:
- click More Symbols
- change the Font dropdown to something like:
    - Times New Roman
    - Arial

- Symbol

Beginner rule:
Try Times New Roman first if you are stuck.

4) Inserting Equations (Basic Beginner Level)
Word 2007 includes an equation tool for basic math formatting.

How to insert an equation
1. Click the **Insert** tab
2. Click **Equation**
3. Choose a built-in equation, or choose **Insert New Equation**
4. Type your equation into the equation box

What you can do inside the equation box:
- fractions
- superscripts (like x^2)
- subscripts (like H_2O)
- square roots

Beginner tip:
If you only need simple math like "2 + 2 = 4," you can type it normally. Use the equation tool when you need proper math formatting.

Practice Example (10 to 15 minutes)
Goal: Insert ±, ©, and a simple equation.

Step 1: Type a short practice page
Open a new document and type this:
Symbols Practice
Temperature change: 3 °C ± 1 °C
Copyright: © 2026 Your Name
Equation: $x^2 + 2x + 1 = 0$
Leave your cursor where you will insert the symbols.

Step 2: Insert the ± symbol
1. Click after the space where ± should appear
2. Insert tab > Symbol > More Symbols
3. Find ±
4. Click Insert
5. Close

Step 3: Insert the © symbol
1. Click where © should appear

2. Insert tab > Symbol > More Symbols
3. Find ©
4. Click Insert
5. Close

Tip:
If you cannot find © quickly, try changing the font list in the symbol box.

Step 4: Insert a simple equation (two options)
Option A (simple typing, acceptable for beginners)
Click after "Equation:" and type:
x^2 + 2x + 1 = 0
This is plain text and is fine for many basic documents.

Option B (use the Equation tool for proper formatting)
1. Place the cursor after "Equation:"
2. Insert tab > Equation > Insert New Equation
3. Type:
   x^2 + 2x + 1 = 0
4. Use the equation tools if you want to convert ^2 into a proper superscript

Expected result:
$x^2 + 2x + 1 = 0$ appears in a neat equation format.

Common beginner problems (quick fixes)
"I cannot find the symbol."
Fix:
- Click More Symbols
- Try a different font (Times New Roman, Arial, Symbol)
- Check the Subset dropdown if available

"The symbol looks different from what I expected."
Fix:
- Change the font of the symbol, or use a common font like Times New Roman

"Equation editing feels confusing."
Fix:
- For now, type simple equations normally
- Use Insert Equation only when you need fractions, roots, or powers that must look formal

Quick check (self-test)

- Where do you insert symbols from in Word 2007?
- What should you do if you cannot find a symbol in the list?
- When should you use the Equation tool instead of typing normally?
- Can Word remember recently used symbols?

PART VI: REFERENCES AND ACADEMIC WORK (REFERENCES TAB)
CHAPTER 1: HEADINGS THAT MAKE LONG DOCUMENTS EASY

Long documents become easy when your headings are clear and consistent. Headings help you organize ideas, move around quickly, and prepare for tools like a Table of Contents later.

This chapter covers:
- heading structure
- using Heading styles correctly
- navigating through headings
- a practice task for turning plain text into a structured document

1) What "Heading Structure" Means

A heading structure is the order and level of headings in your document.

Think of it like this:
- **Heading 1** = main sections
- **Heading 2** = sub-sections under Heading 1
- **Heading 3** = smaller sections under Heading 2 (optional)

Example structure:
- Heading 1: Introduction
  - o Heading 2: Background
  - o Heading 2: Purpose
- Heading 1: Main Discussion
  - o Heading 2: Point One
  - o Heading 2: Point Two
- Heading 1: Conclusion

Beginner rule:
Do not jump levels. If you use Heading 2, it must sit under a Heading 1.

2) Why Headings Make Long Documents Easier

Headings help you:
- break a long text into readable parts
- keep formatting consistent
- find sections quickly
- update the look of all headings at once

- prepare for a Table of Contents and page numbering systems

Beginner rule:

If your document is more than 2 pages, headings are not optional. They are necessary.

3) Apply Headings Using Styles (Not Manual Formatting)

Many beginners make headings by:
- increasing font size
- making text bold
- adding extra spacing with Enter

That looks like headings, but Word does not "understand" them.

The correct method:

Use the built-in styles:
- Heading 1
- Heading 2
- Heading 3

Where:
- **Home tab > Styles group**

4) Navigate Through Headings (Word 2007 Level)

Word 2007 does not have the modern Navigation Pane like newer versions, but you can still navigate effectively.

Method A: Document Map (best for Word 2007)
1. Click the **View** tab
2. Check **Document Map**

A panel appears (usually on the left).

It shows your Heading 1 and Heading 2 structure.

Click a heading in the map to jump to that section.

Method B: Search headings using Find
1. Press **Ctrl + F**
2. Search for a heading word like "Conclusion"
3. Jump through results

Beginner tip:

Document Map becomes powerful only when you use real heading styles.

Practice Example (20 to 30 minutes)

Goal: Convert a 2-page text into headings and sections.

If you already have a 2-page document, use it. If not, use the sample text below and repeat a few paragraphs until it becomes about 2 pages.

Step 1: Create or open your text

Create a new document and paste or type this sample content (you can expand it by adding more sentences):

The Importance of Study Habits

Good study habits help students learn faster and remember more. Many students struggle because they study without a plan.

Why Students Struggle

Some students wait until the last day. Others study for many hours but without focus. Poor sleep and lack of routine also reduce learning.

Planning a Simple Routine

A student can improve by setting study times, reducing distractions, and practicing daily. Even 30 minutes a day can help.

Tools That Help

Simple tools include a notebook, a timetable, and a quiet place. Digital tools like reminders can also help.

Conclusion

Study habits improve results over time. The goal is consistency, not perfection.

Step 2: Identify your headings

Decide what the main sections are. For this practice, use these as Heading 1:

- The Importance of Study Habits
- Why Students Struggle
- Planning a Simple Routine
- Tools That Help
- Conclusion

Step 3: Apply Heading 1

For each main section title:
1. Select the heading line
2. Home tab > Styles group
3. Click **Heading 1**

Step 4: Create and apply Heading 2 (add sub-sections)

Add two subheadings under one section, for practice.

Example under "Why Students Struggle," add:
- Lack of planning
- Distractions

Steps:
1. Place your cursor under "Why Students Struggle" paragraph
2. Type:
   Lack of planning
3. Press Enter, then apply **Heading 2**
4. Type:
   Distractions
5. Press Enter, then apply **Heading 2**
6. Add one short paragraph under each subheading

Step 5: Turn on Document Map and navigate
1. View tab
2. Check **Document Map**
3. Click each heading in the map to jump around your document

Expected result:
You can move through your document by clicking headings, instead of scrolling.

Common beginner problems (quick fixes)
"My headings do not appear in Document Map."
Cause:
You formatted headings manually instead of using Heading styles.
Fix:
Apply Heading 1 and Heading 2 from the Styles group.
"My structure looks confusing."
Fix:
Keep it simple:
- Heading 1 for main sections
- Heading 2 only when you truly need sub-sections

"My headings look too large."
Fix:
Modify the style:
- Right-click Heading 1 > Modify
- Adjust size and spacing
  Do this once, not on every heading.

Quick check (self-test)
- What is the difference between bolding text and applying a Heading style?
- What is Heading 1 used for?
- How do you turn on Document Map in Word 2007?
- Why do headings make long documents easier?

CHAPTER 2: TABLE OF CONTENTS THE CORRECT WAY

A Table of Contents (TOC) is only "correct" when Word builds it from real heading styles. If you type a TOC manually, it becomes wrong the moment page numbers change.

This chapter covers:
- generating a TOC
- updating a TOC
- fixing a broken TOC
- a simple practice task using Heading 1 and Heading 2

1) What Word Needs Before It Can Build a TOC

Word builds a TOC from:
- **Heading 1**
- **Heading 2**
- **Heading 3** (optional)

If your headings are only bold and larger, Word will not recognize them.

Beginner rule:
No heading styles = no correct TOC.

2) How to Generate a Table of Contents (Word 2007)

Step-by-step
1. Click where you want the TOC (usually at the beginning, after the title page)
2. Click the **References** tab
3. Click **Table of Contents**
4. Choose a built-in TOC style (Automatic Table is fine)

Word inserts a TOC that includes:
- heading titles
- page numbers
- dot leaders (the dotted line)

3) How to Update the Table of Contents

Your TOC becomes outdated when:
- text is added or removed
- headings change
- page numbers shift

Update the TOC correctly
1. Click anywhere inside the TOC

2. Click **Update Table** (a button appears above the TOC or on the References tab)

Word will ask what you want to update:
- **Update page numbers only**
- **Update entire table**

Beginner rule:
If you changed heading text, choose "Update entire table."
If you only added text that changed pages, "Update page numbers only" is enough.

4) Fixing a Broken TOC (Common Problems)
Problem A: The TOC does not include some headings
Cause:
Those headings were not styled as Heading 1 or Heading 2.
Fix:
1. Find the missing heading in the document
2. Apply the correct style (Heading 1 or Heading 2)
3. Update the TOC (Update entire table)

Problem B: The TOC text looks messy or has wrong spacing
Cause:
Manual formatting was applied inside the TOC.
Fix:
- Do not manually edit the TOC text.
- Delete the TOC and insert it again, or modify TOC styles properly (advanced).

Beginner rule:
Never type inside the TOC unless you are deleting and rebuilding it.

Problem C: Page numbers are wrong
Cause:
The TOC has not been updated after edits.
Fix:
Click TOC > Update Table > Update page numbers only.

Problem D: The TOC shows strange entries
Cause:
Random text was accidentally formatted as a heading style.
Fix:
- Find that text and change it back to Normal style
- Update the TOC (entire table)

Practice Example (20 minutes)
Goal: Build a TOC from Heading 1 and Heading 2.
Step 1: Create a short structured document
Open a new document and type this content. Press Enter between headings and paragraphs.
My Study Report
Introduction
This report explains my simple study routine and why it works.
Daily Routine
Morning session
I study typing and basic formatting for 30 minutes.
Evening session
I review my notes and correct mistakes.
Tools I Use
Notebook
A notebook helps me plan and track progress.
Phone reminders
Reminders help me stay consistent.
Conclusion
Consistency improves learning over time.
Step 2: Apply heading styles
Apply styles like this:
Heading 1:
- Introduction
- Daily Routine
- Tools I Use
- Conclusion

Heading 2:
- Morning session
- Evening session
- Notebook
- Phone reminders

How:
1. Select the heading line
2. Home tab > Styles
3. Click Heading 1 or Heading 2

Leave normal paragraphs as Normal text.
Step 3: Insert the TOC
1. Click above "Introduction" (after the title) and press Enter to create space

2. Place your cursor where the TOC should go
3. References tab > Table of Contents
4. Choose an automatic style

Step 4: Test updating the TOC
1. Scroll down and add one extra sentence in any paragraph
2. Add a new Heading 2 under "Tools I Use," for example:
   Computer practice
   Then type one sentence under it
3. Go back to the TOC
4. Click inside the TOC
5. Click Update Table
6. Choose **Update entire table**

Expected result:
Your new subheading appears and page numbers adjust.

Common beginner problems (quick fixes)
"My TOC is empty or very short."
Fix:
You did not apply Heading styles. Apply Heading 1 and Heading 2, then update.
"I changed a heading, but the TOC still shows the old one."
Fix:
Update the TOC and choose Update entire table.
"I typed inside the TOC and now it looks broken."
Fix:
Undo (Ctrl + Z). If too late, delete the TOC and insert it again.

Quick check (self-test)
- What must you do before Word can generate a correct TOC?
- Where do you insert a TOC in Word 2007?
- When should you choose "Update entire table"?
- Why should you avoid editing inside the TOC?

CHAPTER 3: FOOTNOTES AND ENDNOTES

Footnotes and endnotes help you add extra information or cite sources without breaking the flow of your main text.

This chapter covers:
- the difference between footnotes and endnotes
- how to insert them
- basic formatting and management
- a short practice task with two footnotes

1) Footnotes vs Endnotes (Simple Difference)

Footnotes

Footnotes appear at the bottom of the same page where the note is used.

Use footnotes when:
- the reader should see the note immediately
- you are writing a report with short explanations or quick citations
- you want notes close to the text

Endnotes

Endnotes appear at the end of the document (or end of a section).

Use endnotes when:
- you want the pages to look cleaner
- you have many notes and want them collected in one place
- the teacher or publisher prefers endnotes

Beginner rule:

If you are not sure which to use, choose footnotes. They are easier to follow while reading.

2) How to Insert a Footnote (Word 2007)

1. Click in your document where the note number should appear (after a word or sentence)
2. Click the **References** tab
3. Click **Insert Footnote**
4. Word jumps to the bottom of the page
5. Type your footnote text
6. Click back in the main text to continue writing

Shortcut note:

Word manages the numbering automatically.

3) How to Insert an Endnote (Word 2007)
1. Click where you want the endnote number
2. References tab
3. Click **Insert Endnote**
4. Word jumps to the endnotes area
5. Type the note
6. Return to your main text

4) Formatting Footnotes and Endnotes (Beginner Level)
Changing number style (1, 2, 3 or i, ii, iii)
1. References tab
2. In the Footnotes group, click the small dialog launcher arrow
3. Choose Number format
4. Click Apply

Moving between notes
- Click the footnote number in the main text to jump to the note
- Click back in the main text to continue

Deleting a footnote correctly
Do not delete the footnote text at the bottom first.
Correct method:
- Delete the footnote number in the main text
  Word removes the footnote automatically.

Beginner rule:
Delete the reference number in the main text, not the footnote text.

Practice Example (20 minutes)
Goal: Add two footnotes to a short report.

Step 1: Type a short report
Open a new Word document and type this:
Mobile data is expensive in many areas, and it affects learning and communication. People often spend money on data that could be used for other basic needs. Some users reduce costs by downloading content during off-peak hours and reading offline.

Step 2: Add Footnote 1
1. Click after the word "expensive" in the first sentence

2. References tab > Insert Footnote
   3. At the bottom of the page, type:
      Data costs vary by location and network provider.

Step 3: Add Footnote 2
   1. Click after the words "off-peak hours" in the last sentence
   2. References tab > Insert Footnote
   3. Type:
      Off-peak hours usually mean late night or early morning, when networks are less busy.

Step 4: Check numbering

You should see:
- a small 1 and 2 in the main text
- matching notes at the bottom of the page

Step 5: Practice deleting one note correctly (optional)
   1. In the main text, delete the footnote number 2
   2. Confirm footnote 2 disappears from the bottom automatically
   3. Press Ctrl + Z if you want to bring it back

Common beginner problems (quick fixes)

"My footnote disappeared."

Cause:

You deleted the footnote number in the main text. That deletes the footnote, which is correct.

Fix:

Press **Ctrl + Z** to undo.

"My numbering looks strange."

Fix:

Open Footnote settings (dialog launcher) and set number format back to 1, 2, 3.

"I cannot find the footnote area."

Fix:

Scroll to the bottom of the page, or double-click the footnote number in the text to jump down.

Quick check (self-test)
- Where do footnotes appear?
- Where do endnotes appear?
- How do you insert a footnote in Word 2007?
- What is the correct way to delete a footnote?

CHAPTER 4: CITATIONS AND BIBLIOGRAPHY BASICS

Word 2007 can help you store sources, insert citations, and generate a bibliography automatically. This works best when you enter your source details correctly from the start.

This chapter covers:
- choosing a citation style
- adding sources
- inserting citations
- generating a bibliography
- a short practice task with one book source and one citation

1) What Word Can Do (Beginner Level)
Word 2007 can:
- save your sources in a list
- insert an in-text citation (example: Author, Year)
- build a bibliography from saved sources

Beginner rule:
If you type citations manually, Word cannot build a bibliography for you.

2) Choose a Citation Style First
Before adding sources, choose a style such as:
- APA
- MLA
- Chicago

How to choose a style:
1. Click the **References** tab
2. Find the **Citations & Bibliography** group
3. Open the **Style** drop-down
4. Choose **APA** (common for many academic papers)

Beginner tip:
If your teacher requires a specific style, choose it before you insert any citations.

3) Add a Source (Book Example)
A source is the full details of a book, website, journal article, or report.

How to add a source:
1. References tab

2. Click **Manage Sources**
3. Click **New**
4. In "Type of Source," choose **Book**
5. Fill in the details (author, title, year, publisher)
6. Click **OK**
7. Click **Close**

Beginner rule:
Enter names and titles carefully. Your bibliography will copy exactly what you type.

4) Insert a Citation (Place It in the Text)
How to insert a citation:
1. Click where the citation should appear in your sentence
2. References tab
3. Click **Insert Citation**
4. Choose the source you added

Word inserts the citation in the correct format for the style you chose.

5) Generate a Bibliography (Automatic List of Sources)
How to create a bibliography:
1. Click where you want the bibliography (usually at the end of the document)
2. References tab
3. Click **Bibliography**
4. Choose Bibliography or Works Cited

Word builds the list automatically from your saved sources.

Beginner rule:
If you add a new source later, you must update the bibliography by deleting and reinserting it, or by updating fields if available.

Practice Example (20 minutes)
Goal: Add one book source and insert one citation.

Step 1: Create a short practice paragraph
Open a new document and type this:
Good study habits improve learning over time, especially when a student follows a consistent routine.
Click at the end of the sentence (where you want the citation).

Step 2: Choose a citation style
1. References tab
2. In Citations & Bibliography, set Style to **APA**

Step 3: Add one book source
1. References tab
2. Manage Sources
3. New
4. Type of Source: **Book**

Fill with a sample book (for practice):
- Author: James Clear
- Title: Atomic Habits
- Year: 2018
- Publisher: Avery

Click OK, then Close.

Step 4: Insert the citation
1. Click at the end of your sentence
2. References tab
3. Insert Citation
4. Choose the book source you added

Expected result:
You will see an APA-style citation inserted (example: Clear, 2018).

Step 5: Add a bibliography at the end
1. Press Enter a few times to go to a new line
2. Type: Bibliography
3. Press Enter
4. References tab
5. Bibliography
6. Choose **Bibliography**

Expected result:
Word inserts a formatted bibliography entry for the book.

Common beginner problems (quick fixes)
"My source is not showing up in Insert Citation."
Fix:
- Open Manage Sources and confirm the source is in the Current List
- If it is in Master List, copy it to Current List

"The bibliography looks wrong."

Cause:
The source details were typed incorrectly.
Fix:
- Manage Sources > select the source > Edit
- Correct the details, then rebuild the bibliography

"My teacher uses a different style."
Fix:
Change the Style dropdown before inserting citations. If you already inserted citations, changing the style may update them, but always double-check.

Quick check (self-test)
- Why should you choose a citation style first?
- Where do you add a new source in Word 2007?
- How do you insert a citation into a sentence?
- How does Word build a bibliography?

CHAPTER 5: CAPTIONS AND CROSS-REFERENCES

Captions and cross-references are what make academic and professional documents feel polished. They help you label tables and figures properly, and they let Word update references automatically if numbering changes later.

This chapter covers:
- adding captions to tables and figures
- inserting cross-references that update
- updating fields
- a practice task: caption a table and cross-reference it in the text

1) What a Caption Is (And Why It Matters)

A caption is a label Word adds to a table, figure, or image, such as:
- Table 1: Daily Timetable
- Figure 1: Process Diagram

Captions matter because:
- Word can number them automatically
- Word can create a Table of Figures later
- You can cross-reference them correctly in your writing

Beginner rule:
Do not type "Table 1" manually. Let Word generate it.

2) Insert Captions (Word 2007)

Caption a table
1. Click inside the table (or click the table border)
2. Go to the **References** tab
3. Click **Insert Caption**
4. In Label, choose **Table**
5. In Caption text, type a clear title after the number, for example:
   Daily Timetable
6. Choose Position:
- Above selected item (common for tables)
7. Click OK

Caption a figure (picture, chart, SmartArt)
Same steps, but choose Label: **Figure**.

Beginner tip:
If "Table" or "Figure" is not available as a label:

- Click New Label and type Table or Figure once.

3) Cross-References (References That Update)
A cross-reference is a link inside your text that points to a captioned item.
Example sentence:
See Table 1 for the daily timetable.
If you later insert a new table above it, your original Table 1 becomes Table 2.
With a cross-reference, Word updates the number automatically.
Beginner rule:
Cross-reference is safer than typing table numbers by hand.

4) Insert a Cross-Reference (Word 2007)
1. Click where you want the reference to appear in your text
2. References tab
3. Click **Cross-reference**
4. Reference type: choose **Table** (or Figure)
5. Insert reference to: choose what you want, such as:
- Only label and number (example: Table 1)
- Page number
- Entire caption text
6. Select the correct table from the list
7. Click Insert
8. Click Close

5) Update Captions and Cross-References
Sometimes references do not update immediately.
To update:
- Select the whole document: **Ctrl + A**
- Update fields: press **F9**

Beginner note:
On some laptops, you may need **Fn + F9**.

Practice Example (20 to 25 minutes)
Goal: Caption a table and cross-reference it in text.
Step 1: Create a short paragraph and a table
Open a new document and type this paragraph:

This report includes a small timetable. See Table 1 for the schedule.
Press Enter twice.
Now insert a simple table:
1. Insert tab > Table
2. Choose 3 columns and 4 rows
3. Fill it like this:

Time | Activity | Notes
8:00 | Study | Typing practice
10:00 | Break | Rest
11:00 | Word | Formatting

Step 2: Add a caption to the table
1. Click inside the table
2. References tab > Insert Caption
3. Label: Table
4. Caption title: Daily Timetable
5. Position: Above selected item
6. OK

You should now see something like:
Table 1: Daily Timetable

Step 3: Replace the manual "Table 1" in your paragraph with a cross-reference
1. In the first paragraph, delete the typed "Table 1" only
2. Click where "Table 1" should be
3. References tab > Cross-reference
4. Reference type: Table
5. Insert reference to: Only label and number
6. Select your captioned table
7. Insert > Close

Now your sentence becomes:
See Table 1 for the schedule.
But the "Table 1" is now a cross-reference.

Step 4: Test that it updates
1. Above your table, insert another new table (a small 2x2 table is fine)
2. Add a caption to the new table too
3. Your timetable may become Table 2 now

Update everything:
1. Ctrl + A
2. F9

Expected result:
The cross-reference in your paragraph updates to the new number automatically.

Common beginner problems (quick fixes)
"Cross-reference list is empty."
Cause:
You did not insert a caption first.
Fix:
Insert a caption, then try Cross-reference again.
"The cross-reference number did not change."
Fix:
Update fields:
- Ctrl + A, then F9

"I typed inside the caption and broke the numbering."
Fix:
Undo (Ctrl + Z).
If needed, delete the caption and insert it again using Insert Caption.

Quick check (self-test)
- What is a caption used for?
- Why is a cross-reference better than typing "Table 1" manually?
- Where do you insert a caption in Word 2007?
- What keys update all cross-references in a document?

CHAPTER 6: INDEX AND TABLE OF AUTHORITIES (OPTIONAL)

Most beginners do not need an Index or a Table of Authorities. But it helps to understand what they are, so you know when to use them and when to skip them.

This chapter covers:
- what an index is
- what a table of authorities is
- when to skip them
- a small practice task: a tiny index with 5 terms

1) What an Index Is

An index is an alphabetical list of important terms at the end of a document, with page numbers.

Example:
Formatting, 3, 7
Headings, 10, 12
Tables, 15

Indexes are common in:
- textbooks
- reference books
- manuals
- long reports with many terms

Beginner rule:
If your document is under 20 pages, you can usually skip an index.

2) What a Table of Authorities Is

A Table of Authorities is a special list used in legal documents. It collects:
- cases
- statutes
- legal citations

It is common in:
- legal briefs
- court documents
- legal research writing

Beginner rule:
If you are not writing legal documents, you can skip Table of Authorities completely.

3) When Beginners Should Skip These Tools
Skip Index and Table of Authorities when:
- you are writing school assignments under 10 to 15 pages
- you are writing a normal report, letter, or essay
- you are still learning headings and table of contents (these are more important)

Use Index when:
- your document is long
- it contains many repeated key terms
- you want readers to find topics quickly

4) How an Index Works (Simple Explanation)
Creating an index has two main steps:
1. Mark the terms inside your document (tell Word what to index)
2. Insert the index at the end (Word builds it with page numbers)

Beginner note:
Marking entries is the main work. Word can only build an index from terms you mark.

Practice Example (25 to 30 minutes)
Goal: Create a tiny index with 5 terms.

Step 1: Create a short practice document
Open a new Word document and type this short text (you can add extra sentences to make it longer):

Microsoft Word 2007 helps beginners write documents. Good formatting makes text easier to read. Headings help structure long documents. Tables organize information clearly. Citations support academic work. Captions label tables and figures.

Press Enter a few times and type the same sentences again in a different order. This helps make sure terms appear more than once.

Step 2: Choose 5 terms to index
Use these terms:
- Word
- formatting
- headings
- tables

- citations

Step 3: Mark each index entry
For each term, do the following:
1. Highlight the term in the text (example: highlight "formatting")
2. Go to **References** tab
3. Click **Mark Entry**
4. In the box, confirm the main entry looks correct
5. Click **Mark**

Repeat for all five terms.

Beginner tip:
If the term appears more than once and you want all instances indexed:
- Use **Mark All** instead of Mark
  But for practice, Mark is enough.

Step 4: Insert the index at the end
1. Press **Ctrl + End** to go to the end of the document
2. Press Enter a few times
3. Type:
   Index
4. Press Enter
5. References tab > **Insert Index**
6. Click OK

Expected result:
Word inserts an alphabetical index with page numbers.

How to See Index Marks (So You Understand What Happened)
Word inserts hidden codes like:
- XE "formatting"

To see them:
- Home tab > click **Show/Hide** (¶)

Beginner warning:
Do not delete index codes unless you know what you are doing. If you remove them, the index can break.

Common beginner problems (quick fixes)
"My index is empty."
Cause:
You did not mark any entries.

Fix:
Mark at least a few terms, then insert the index again.
"The index page numbers are wrong."
Fix:
Update fields:
- Ctrl + A, then F9

"I see strange XE codes in my document."
Fix:
Turn off Show/Hide (¶). The codes are normal.

Quick check (self-test)
- What is an index used for?
- Who usually needs a Table of Authorities?
- What must you do before Word can generate an index?
- How do you update an index after changes?

PART VII: PAGE LAYOUT TOOLS (PAGE LAYOUT TAB)
CHAPTER 1: THEMES AND BASIC DOCUMENT LOOK

Themes help you change the overall look of a document quickly. A theme can apply a matching set of fonts, colors, and effects so the document feels consistent.

This chapter covers:
- what a theme changes
- when to use themes (and when not to)
- how to apply a theme
- how to revert safely
- a short practice task

1) What a Theme Is

A theme is a packaged design set that can change:
- theme fonts (heading and body fonts)
- theme colors (used for shapes, SmartArt, charts, some highlights)
- theme effects (visual effects for shapes and objects)

Beginner note:
A theme does not usually change every single part of plain text the way beginners expect. It mainly affects headings, objects, and styles that use theme fonts and theme colors.

2) When Themes Are Useful

Themes are useful for:
- simple reports that need a clean consistent look
- newsletters and handouts
- documents with headings, SmartArt, and charts
- quick design consistency without manual formatting

Themes are not ideal for:
- formal academic papers with strict formatting rules
- documents where your school or office requires a specific font (example: Times New Roman 12)
- documents that must match a company template

Beginner rule:
If your teacher or office specifies a font and size, follow that requirement first.

3) Where Themes Are Found

Themes are in:
- **Page Layout** tab
- **Themes** group

You will see:
- Themes
- Colors
- Fonts
- Effects

4) How to Apply a Theme (Safe Beginner Method)
Before changing themes:
- Save your document (Ctrl + S)

Then:
1. Go to **Page Layout**
2. Click **Themes**
3. Hover over a theme to preview (if preview works)
4. Click a theme to apply it

Beginner tip:
If you do not like the result, undo immediately:
- Ctrl + Z

5) Reverting Safely (Getting Back to Normal)
Method A: Undo (best right away)
- Press **Ctrl + Z**

Method B: Reapply the original theme
If Undo is not available or you changed many things:
1. Page Layout tab
2. Themes
3. Choose the default theme (often "Office" or "Office 2007" depending on your setup)

Method C: Reset theme colors and fonts separately
If only colors or fonts look wrong:
- Page Layout > Colors > choose the default
- Page Layout > Fonts > choose the default

Beginner rule:
Undo is the fastest safe revert. Use it immediately when possible.

Practice Example (15 minutes)
Goal: Apply a theme and revert safely.

Step 1: Create a small sample document
Open a new Word document and type:
Theme Practice Document
Introduction
This document is used to practice themes in Word 2007.
Key Points
Themes can change fonts and colors. Use them carefully.
Conclusion
If a theme makes the document look wrong, you can undo or revert.

Step 2: Apply heading styles (so you can see theme changes clearly)
1. Select "Theme Practice Document" and apply **Heading 1**
2. Select "Introduction," "Key Points," and "Conclusion" and apply **Heading 2**

This makes the theme effects obvious.

Step 3: Save your document
- Press **Ctrl + S**
  Save it as:
  Theme Practice.docx

Step 4: Apply a theme
1. Page Layout tab
2. Click Themes
3. Choose any theme

Notice what changes:
- headings may change fonts
- colors for headings or lines may change
- SmartArt or shapes (if any) would change colors

Step 5: Revert safely
Method A:
- Press **Ctrl + Z** once or twice until the theme is removed

Method B (if needed):
1. Page Layout tab
2. Themes
3. Choose the default "Office" theme (or the original theme)

Common beginner problems (quick fixes)

"Nothing changed when I applied a theme."
Reason:
Your text is mostly Normal style and uses manual formatting.
Fix:
Use heading styles, shapes, or SmartArt to see theme changes clearly.

"My fonts changed but I want Times New Roman."
Fix:
Do not use themes for that document, or set fonts back:
- Page Layout > Fonts > choose a font set that matches your requirement
  Or manually set your styles back.

"My document now looks confusing."
Fix:
Undo, or apply the default theme again.

Quick check (self-test)
- What three main things can a theme change?
- Where do you find Themes in Word 2007?
- What is the fastest way to revert a theme change?
- When should you avoid themes?

CHAPTER 2: INDENTS, SPACING, AND LAYOUT CONTROLS

Many documents look inconsistent because paragraphs have mixed spacing and random indents. Word 2007 lets you control these settings from the Page Layout tab so your layout stays uniform across the whole document.

This chapter covers:
- indents and spacing controls on the Page Layout tab
- how to keep layout consistent
- a practice task: standardize spacing across a 3-page document

1) Why Layout Consistency Matters

Consistent layout means:
- headings look uniform
- paragraphs have the same spacing
- the document looks professional
- printing is predictable

Beginner rule:
If your document looks messy, fix spacing and indents before changing fonts or colors.

2) Where Page Layout Paragraph Controls Are Found

Go to:
- **Page Layout tab**
- **Paragraph group**

You will see:
- Indent: Left, Right
- Spacing: Before, After

These are quick controls. They affect the selected paragraph(s).

Beginner note:
These controls are the same paragraph settings you also see on the Home tab, just presented differently.

3) Indents (Left and Right)

Left indent

Moves the whole paragraph away from the left margin.
Use left indent for:
- block quotes
- nested notes
- special formatting (rare)

Right indent
Moves the paragraph away from the right margin.
Use right indent for:
- special layout needs (rare)

Beginner warning:
Random indents are a common mistake. If text starts too far in, check left indent first.

4) Spacing (Before and After)
Spacing Before/After controls the blank space around paragraphs without pressing Enter.
Use spacing for:
- separating paragraphs cleanly
- creating space after headings
- improving readability

Beginner rule:
Do not create spacing by pressing Enter many times. Use Before/After spacing.

5) The Clean Standard (A Simple Default You Can Use)
If you do not have a required school format, a clean default is:
Normal paragraphs:
- Line spacing: 1.15 or 1.5
- Spacing Before: 0 pt
- Spacing After: 6 pt or 8 pt
- Left indent: 0
- Right indent: 0

Headings:
- Slightly more spacing before (example: 12 pt)
- Moderate spacing after (example: 6 pt)

Beginner rule:
Pick one standard and apply it everywhere.

6) The Best Way to Standardize Layout (Beginner-Friendly)
You have two beginner-safe approaches:
Approach A: Standardize manually using Page Layout controls
Good when:
- the document is short
- you just want quick cleanup

Approach B: Use Styles (best long-term)
Good when:
- the document is long
- you want consistency automatically
- you want Table of Contents and clean formatting later

For this practice, you will use Approach A and a simple style check.

Practice Example (25 to 35 minutes)
Goal: Standardize spacing across a 3-page document.
If you do not have a 3-page document, create one by copying a paragraph and pasting it many times until it reaches 3 pages.

Step 1: Turn on Show/Hide (optional but helpful)
1. Home tab
2. Click **Show/Hide** (¶)

This helps you see extra blank lines and formatting marks.

Step 2: Select the whole document
- Press **Ctrl + A**

Step 3: Reset the indents to normal
1. Go to **Page Layout** tab
2. In Paragraph group:
- Set Left indent to **0**
- Set Right indent to **0**

Step 4: Standardize paragraph spacing (Before and After)
With everything still selected:
1. Page Layout tab
2. Paragraph group:
- Set **Spacing Before** to **0 pt**
- Set **Spacing After** to **6 pt** (or 8 pt)

This immediately makes paragraph gaps consistent.

Step 5: Standardize line spacing
Line spacing is not in the Page Layout quick boxes. Use the Home tab for this step.
1. Keep everything selected (Ctrl + A if needed)
2. Home tab > Paragraph group
3. Click Line Spacing
4. Choose **1.15** or **1.5** (choose one)

Step 6: Remove extra blank lines (common beginner cleanup)
If you see many empty lines (multiple ¶ marks):

- Place your cursor in the area
- Delete extra empty paragraphs until spacing looks normal

Beginner rule:
Use spacing settings, not extra Enter presses.

Step 7: Fix headings separately (simple method)
Headings often need different spacing than normal paragraphs. Do this:
1. Click one heading
2. Apply a heading style (Heading 1 or Heading 2) from Home tab > Styles
3. Repeat for other headings

Optional:
If headings look too far apart after your spacing changes:
- Select headings only
- Reduce Spacing After to 0 pt or 3 pt, and set Spacing Before to 12 pt

How to Check You Succeeded
Your document should now have:
- equal paragraph spacing everywhere
- no random indents
- consistent line spacing
- headings clearly separated from body text
- fewer blank lines created by Enter

Quick test:
Scroll quickly from page 1 to page 3. The spacing should look uniform, not random.

Common beginner problems (quick fixes)
"My headings now look like normal text."
Fix:
Reapply Heading styles to headings. Styles override many manual settings.

"Everything looks too spaced out."
Fix:
Reduce:
- line spacing (try 1.15)
- spacing after (try 6 pt instead of 8 pt)

"Some paragraphs still look different."

Cause:
Some text has direct formatting applied.
Fix:
Select the paragraph and use:
- Home tab > Clear Formatting
  Then reapply your spacing standard.

Quick check (self-test)
- Where do you find Indent and Spacing controls on the Page Layout tab?
- Why is Spacing Before/After better than pressing Enter many times?
- What are two settings that standardize most documents quickly?
- When is it better to use Styles instead of manual cleanup?

CHAPTER 3: PAGE BORDERS AND WATERMARK FOR OFFICIAL DOCUMENTS

Page borders and watermarks can make a document look official, but they can also make it look unprofessional if used without a clear reason. This chapter shows how to use them correctly and when to avoid them.

This chapter covers:
- professional use of page borders
- professional use of watermarks
- when to avoid both
- a practice task: add and remove a "DRAFT" watermark

1) Page Borders (Professional Use)

A page border is a line or frame around the edge of the page.

When page borders are appropriate
- certificates
- formal letters for special occasions (if required by the organization)
- official notices or announcements
- school projects where design is expected (not strict academic papers)

When page borders should be avoided
- academic research papers (usually)
- business reports where simplicity is preferred
- documents that will be copied many times (borders can degrade)
- documents printed on different printers (borders may be cut off)

Beginner rule:
If the document is serious and formal, keep borders simple or skip them completely.

2) Watermarks (Professional Use)

A watermark is faint text behind the page content, like:
- DRAFT
- CONFIDENTIAL
- SAMPLE
- INTERNAL USE ONLY

When watermarks are appropriate

- draft documents shared for review
- training materials
- internal office documents
- documents that must not be mistaken for final versions

When watermarks should be avoided
- final official letters
- final academic submissions
- documents where watermark makes reading harder

Beginner rule:
Use watermarks only when it protects against confusion (draft vs final).

3) Where Borders and Watermarks Are Found (Word 2007)

Go to:
- **Page Layout** tab

Then:
- **Page Borders**
- **Watermark**

4) How to Add a Watermark ("DRAFT")

1. Click the **Page Layout** tab
2. Click **Watermark**
3. Choose **DRAFT** (built-in option)

If you do not see DRAFT:
1. Page Layout > Watermark
2. Click **Custom Watermark**
3. Choose **Text watermark**
4. Type: DRAFT
5. Choose a light color and a diagonal layout (common)
6. Click OK

5) How to Remove a Watermark

1. Page Layout tab
2. Watermark
3. Click **Remove Watermark**

Beginner note:
If you used a custom watermark and it does not remove properly, it is still removed through Remove Watermark. If it

remains, it may be placed as a header object, and you can delete it by opening the header.

Practice Example (10 to 15 minutes)
Goal: Add a watermark "DRAFT" and remove it.
Step 1: Create a short draft document
Open a new Word document and type:
Draft Report
This is a draft document for review. Please check formatting and spelling before final submission.
Save it:
- Ctrl + S
  Name it:
  Draft Practice.docx

Step 2: Add the "DRAFT" watermark
1. Page Layout tab
2. Watermark
3. Choose **DRAFT**

Check:
- The word DRAFT should appear faintly behind your text.

Step 3: Remove the watermark
1. Page Layout tab
2. Watermark
3. Click **Remove Watermark**

Check:
- The watermark disappears.

Common beginner problems (quick fixes)
"My watermark is too dark."
Fix:
Use Custom Watermark and choose a lighter color.
"My border is cut off when printing."
Fix:
Remove the border or increase margins. Printer margins vary.
"I cannot remove the watermark."
Fix:
- Use Page Layout > Watermark > Remove Watermark
  If it still appears:

117

- Double-click the header area and see if the watermark object is placed there, then delete it.

Quick check (self-test)
- When is a watermark useful in a professional document?
- Where do you add a watermark in Word 2007?
- How do you remove a watermark?
- Why should you avoid page borders in many formal documents?

PART VIII: MAILINGS FOR BEGINNERS (MAILINGS TAB)
CHAPTER 1: ENVELOPES AND LABELS

The Mailings tab helps you prepare envelopes and labels for printing. Beginners often use it for:
- sending letters
- printing address labels
- creating name labels for files or folders

This chapter covers:
- setting up an envelope
- setting up labels
- safe printing habits (test first)
- a practice task: print one label on plain paper for testing

1) Envelopes (Basic Use)
What an envelope setup does
Word can place:
- the delivery address
- the return address

in the correct position for printing on an envelope.

Where to find envelope tools
1. Click the **Mailings** tab
2. In the Create group, click **Envelopes**

How to set up an envelope
1. Mailings tab > Envelopes
2. Type the Delivery address
3. Type the Return address (optional)
4. Click **Options** if you need to choose envelope size
5. Click:
- Print (to print directly), or
- Add to Document (to place it in a Word file)

Beginner tip:
Printing envelopes can be tricky because every printer feeds envelopes differently. Test with a blank envelope first.

2) Labels (Basic Use)
Labels are small printed blocks, often used for addresses.
Where to find labels
1. Mailings tab
2. Click **Labels**

Word can create:
- a full page of labels, or
- a single label

3) The Safe Printing Method (Always Test First)
Beginner rule:
Always test on plain paper before using real label sheets.
Why:
- label sheets are expensive
- a wrong printer setting wastes the whole sheet
- printer alignment can be off

Practice Example (15 to 20 minutes)
Goal: Print one label on plain paper for testing.
Step 1: Open the Labels tool
1. Open Word 2007
2. Click the **Mailings** tab
3. Click **Labels**

Step 2: Type your test label text
In the Address box, type something like:
Your Name
Your Address
City, Country
Phone Number
This is only for practice.

Step 3: Choose a single label
1. Under Print, choose **Single label**
2. Set:
- Row: 1
- Column: 1

This prints only the top-left label spot.

Step 4: Choose a label vendor and product number (important)
1. Click **Options**
2. Label vendors:
   Choose a common vendor listed there (example: Avery)
3. Product number:
   Choose any standard address label product number (for practice)

Beginner tip:
If you do not know your label sheet number yet, choose a common address label option for practice. The main goal is learning the steps.
Click OK.

Step 5: Print on plain paper (test)
1. Load plain paper in the printer
2. Click **Print**
3. In the print settings:
   - Make sure the correct printer is selected
   - Print only 1 copy

Check the result:
- You should see your test label printed near the top-left area of the page.

Step 6: Confirm alignment
Hold the printed plain paper behind a real label sheet (do not peel labels).
Check if the printed text would land inside the label area.
If it is off:
- adjust by selecting the correct label product number
- check printer settings and paper size (Letter vs A4)

Common beginner problems (quick fixes)
"My text prints in the wrong place."
Fix:
- confirm the label product number matches your label sheet
- confirm paper size matches your label sheet (Letter or A4)

"Nothing prints."
Fix:
- confirm the correct printer is selected
- confirm printer is on and connected
- try printing a normal document to test the printer

"The text is too close to label edges."
Fix:
- reduce font size slightly
- shorten lines
- choose the correct label template in Options

Quick check (self-test)
- Where do you find Labels in Word 2007?
- Why should you test on plain paper first?
- What does "Single label" do?
- What is the most common reason label alignment is wrong?

CHAPTER 2: MAIL MERGE STEP BY STEP

Mail Merge lets you create many documents at once, using one template and a list of names and addresses. Beginners use it for:

- letters to many people
- address labels
- simple lists for printing

This chapter covers:

- mail merge for letters and labels
- selecting recipients
- inserting merge fields
- generating the final documents
- a practice task: create 5 letters from a small address list

1) What Mail Merge Does (Simple Explanation)

Mail Merge combines:

1. A main document (your letter template)
2. A recipient list (names and addresses)

Result:
Word produces one letter for each person automatically.
Beginner rule:
Do not type names one by one. Let Mail Merge fill them in.

2) What You Need Before You Start

You need:

- a simple letter template
- a recipient list (can be typed in Word during setup)

Typical fields:

- First Name
- Last Name
- Address
- City
- Phone (optional)

3) Start Mail Merge (Letters)

1. Open Word 2007
2. Click the **Mailings** tab
3. Click **Start Mail Merge**
4. Choose **Letters**

Beginner tip:
Letters are the easiest way to learn mail merge. Labels come later using the same idea.

4) Select Recipients (Create a Small List)
1. Mailings tab
2. Click **Select Recipients**
3. Choose **Type New List**
4. Click **Customize Columns** if you want to remove fields you do not need
5. Enter your five sample recipients
6. Click OK and save the list when Word asks (save it in Documents)

Beginner note:
Word saves this list as a file you can reuse later.

5) Insert Merge Fields (Placeholders)
Merge fields are placeholders like:
- «First_Name»
- «Last_Name»
- «Address»
- «City»

You insert them where you want information to appear.
Where to insert them:
- Mailings tab > **Insert Merge Field**

Beginner rule:
Type the normal words first (like "Dear"), then insert the merge field.

6) Preview Results (Check Before Printing)
Before finishing:
1. Click **Preview Results**
2. Use the arrows (Next/Previous) to check each recipient
3. Confirm names and addresses appear correctly

Beginner rule:
Always preview. It prevents embarrassing mistakes.

7) Finish and Merge (Create the Letters)
To create your letters:

1. Click **Finish & Merge**
2. Choose **Edit Individual Documents**
3. Choose:
- All (to create all letters)
4. Click OK

Word creates a new document with one letter per page.
Beginner tip:
Choose "Edit Individual Documents" first, not Print, because it lets you review before printing.

Practice Example (30 to 40 minutes)
Goal: Create 5 letters from a small address list.
Step 1: Start a new letter document
Open a new Word document.
Type this simple letter template:
Your Organization Name
Your Address
City, Country
Date: February 3, 2026
Dear FirstName,
Thank you for your support. This letter is a quick message to confirm that your details are in our records. Please contact us if anything needs correction.
Sincerely,
Your Name
Important:
Do not type real names yet. You will insert merge fields.
Step 2: Start Mail Merge
1. Mailings tab
2. Start Mail Merge > Letters

Step 3: Create a recipient list of 5 people
1. Mailings tab
2. Select Recipients > Type New List
3. Enter five sample people like these (you can change them):

John | Deng | 123 Main Street | Juba
Mary | Ajak | 45 Market Road | Bor
Peter | James | 10 River Lane | Malakal
Sarah | Lado | 77 Central Ave | Yei
David | Gai | 9 Hill Street | Nimule

4. Click OK
5. Save the list when prompted (example: MyRecipients)

Step 4: Insert merge fields into the letter

Replace "Dear FirstName," with:
1. Click after the word "Dear" and add a space
2. Mailings tab > Insert Merge Field > First Name
3. Add a space
4. Insert Merge Field > Last Name
5. Type a comma

It should look like:

Dear «First Name» «Last Name»,

Optional:

Add address fields at the top if you want a full letter format:
- Insert «Address»
- Insert «City»

But keep it simple for this first practice.

Step 5: Preview the results
1. Click Preview Results
2. Use Next/Previous arrows to view all 5 letters
3. Confirm names appear correctly

Step 6: Finish the merge into a new document
1. Finish & Merge
2. Edit Individual Documents
3. All
4. OK

Expected result:

A new document appears with 5 pages, each page addressed to one person.

Step 7: Save your merged letters

Save the final document as:

Merged Letters.docx

Common beginner problems (quick fixes)

"My fields show the same person every time."

Fix:

Use Preview Results arrows to confirm. If still wrong, check the recipient list selection under Select Recipients.

"I cannot find my saved list."

Fix:

When Select Recipients is used again, choose:

- Use Existing List
  Then browse to where you saved it (Documents is common).

"Some names are blank."
Fix:
Your recipient list may have missing values. Edit the list:
- Edit Recipient List (Mailings tab)

Quick check (self-test)
- What two things does Mail Merge combine?
- Where do you create or select a recipient list?
- What does Preview Results help you do?
- Why should beginners choose "Edit Individual Documents" before printing?

CHAPTER 3: CLEANING RECIPIENT LISTS

Mail merge works best when your recipient list is clean. A "dirty" list causes common problems:
- wrong names
- missing fields
- duplicate letters
- inconsistent formatting (JOHN vs John vs john)
- wrong addresses or cities

This chapter covers:
- sorting
- filtering
- fixing duplicates
- formatting names consistently
- a practice task: filter recipients by city or category

1) What "Cleaning" Means for a Recipient List

A clean recipient list has:
- one person per row
- consistent spelling and capitalization
- no duplicates (unless you want duplicates)
- correct city/category values
- no extra spaces at the start or end of fields

Beginner rule:
If your mail merge output looks wrong, the list is usually the problem.

2) Sorting Recipients (Put the List in Order)

Sorting rearranges the list so it is easier to check.
Common sorting examples:
- by Last Name (A to Z)
- by City
- by Category (Members, Donors, Students)

How to sort in Mail Merge
1. Mailings tab
2. Edit Recipient List
3. Click **Sort**
4. Choose a field (example: City or Last Name)
5. Choose Ascending (A to Z)
6. OK

Beginner tip:
Sorting by City helps you quickly find duplicates and spelling errors.

3) Filtering Recipients (Select Only Some People)
Filtering lets you print letters for a subset of recipients. Examples:
- only people in Juba
- only "Donors" category
- only those with a phone number filled in

How to filter in Mail Merge
1. Mailings tab
2. Edit Recipient List
3. Click **Filter**
4. Choose a field and condition:
- Field: City
- Comparison: Equal to
- Value: Juba
5. OK

Now Word merges only the filtered recipients.
Beginner rule:
Filter before you finish and merge.

4) Fix Duplicates (Stop Sending Two Letters)
Duplicates happen when:
- the same person is entered twice
- the same address is repeated
- names are spelled slightly differently

Beginner-level ways to handle duplicates in Word 2007:
- sort by Last Name or Address, then look for repeats
- remove extra entries in the list
- standardize spelling first, then check again

Where to remove duplicates:
- Mailings tab > Edit Recipient List
- uncheck a duplicate row to exclude it, or edit the source list

Beginner tip:
If the list is large, it is easier to clean it in Excel. But for beginners, learning the Word method is enough.

5) Format Names Consistently (JOHN vs John vs john)
You can clean names in two ways:
Method A: Fix names in the list (best)
Open the recipient list and edit:
- change "JOHN" to "John"
- remove extra spaces
- correct spelling

Method B: Format during mail merge (quick fix)
If a name is in the list as JOHN and you cannot edit the list easily, you can still format in the document using Word's field formatting (advanced for beginners). For now, focus on Method A.
Beginner rule:
Fix the list, not the letter. That prevents the same problem in future merges.

Practice Example (20 to 30 minutes)
Goal: Filter recipients by city or category.
You need a mail merge document connected to a recipient list. If you do not have one, create a simple list first (same method as the previous chapter).

Step 1: Create a sample list with a City and Category field
If your list does not have Category, add it when creating the list:
- Mailings > Select Recipients > Type New List
- Customize Columns > Add "Category"

Enter 8 sample recipients like this:
John | Deng | Juba | Donor
Mary | Ajak | Bor | Member
Peter | James | Juba | Member
Sarah | Lado | Yei | Donor
David | Gai | Juba | Staff
Agnes | Wani | Yei | Member
Paul | Riek | Bor | Donor
Lily | John | Juba | Member
Save the list.

Step 2: Open Edit Recipient List
1. Mailings tab
2. Click **Edit Recipient List**

Step 3: Filter by City (example: Juba)

1. In the list window, click **Filter**
2. Field: City
3. Comparison: Equal to
4. Value: Juba
5. OK

Now only recipients in Juba are included.

Step 4: Preview and confirm
1. Click **Preview Results**
2. Use Next/Previous arrows
3. Confirm only Juba recipients appear

Step 5: Remove the filter (show all recipients again)
1. Mailings tab
2. Edit Recipient List
3. Click Filter
4. Clear the filter (or set it to show all)

Step 6: Filter by Category (example: Donor)
Repeat the filtering steps, but choose:
- Field: Category
- Value: Donor

Common beginner problems (quick fixes)
"Filter does not work."
Fix:
Check spelling. "Juba" is different from "JUBA" if your list is inconsistent. Standardize the list first.

"Some recipients disappeared and I do not know why."
Fix:
You may have an active filter.
Go to Edit Recipient List and clear filters.

"Duplicates still appear."
Fix:
Sort by Last Name or Address, then uncheck duplicate rows in Edit Recipient List, or edit the list to remove them.

Quick check (self-test)
- What does sorting help you do?
- What does filtering help you do?
- Where do you filter recipients in Word 2007?
- Why is it better to fix formatting in the recipient list instead of the letter?

PART IX: REVIEW TOOLS (REVIEW TAB)
CHAPTER 1: SPELLING AND GRAMMAR TOOLS

Spelling and grammar tools can save you time, but they are not always correct. The goal is to use them wisely: trust the tool for obvious spelling mistakes, but double-check grammar suggestions and meaning.

This chapter covers:
- how to run spelling and grammar
- what to trust
- what to double-check
- a practice task: fix 10 errors correctly

1) What Spelling and Grammar Can and Cannot Do
Spelling check is strong at:
- catching misspelled words
- catching repeated typos
- spotting accidental double words (sometimes)

Grammar check is weaker at:
- meaning and tone
- proper names and local place names
- correct grammar in complex sentences
- words that are spelled correctly but used wrongly (example: their vs there)

Beginner rule:
Spelling is usually reliable. Grammar suggestions need your judgment.

2) How to Run Spelling and Grammar (Word 2007)
Method A: Review tab
1. Click the **Review** tab
2. Click **Spelling & Grammar**

Method B: Keyboard shortcut
- Press **F7**

Word will move through the document and show suggestions.

3) Understanding Underlines in Word 2007
Word marks issues as you type:
- red underline: spelling issue
- green underline: grammar issue

Beginner tip:
Right-click an underlined word to see suggestions quickly.

4) What to Trust (Most of the Time)
Trust Word when:
- the word is clearly misspelled
- you see an obvious typo
- the correction matches the meaning you intended

Examples:
- "documant" should be "document"
- "recieve" should be "receive"

5) What to Double-Check (Always)
Double-check Word when:
- it suggests changing your sentence structure
- it flags a proper name (person, place, organization)
- it flags technical terms
- it suggests a word that changes your meaning
- it flags a sentence that is correct but not common

Examples:
- names like Nyakueth, Juba, Malakal
- technical words like toolbar, clipboard, SmartArt

Beginner rule:
If it is a name or a technical word, verify before changing.

6) Basic Buttons You Will See During Review
When the Spelling and Grammar window appears, you commonly see:
- Change
- Change All
- Ignore Once
- Ignore All
- Add to Dictionary

Beginner rules:
- Use Change for one-time corrections
- Use Change All only when you are 100% sure
- Use Add to Dictionary only for correct words you will reuse (names, technical terms)

- Use Ignore for words that are correct but not recognized

Practice Example (20 to 30 minutes)
Goal: Run spelling and grammar, then fix 10 errors correctly.
Step 1: Create a practice paragraph with mistakes
Open a new Word document and type this exactly as written:
Microsft Word helps you write documants fast. It has a ribon with many tools. You can creat files, save them, and printt them. When you make mistaks, you can use Undo. Word can also chekc spelling and grammer, but you must be carefull. Some sugestions are wrong, especialy for names and tecnical words.
This paragraph contains more than 10 mistakes.
Step 2: Run Spelling and Grammar
1. Press **F7**
   or
2. Review tab > Spelling & Grammar

Step 3: Fix errors correctly (one by one)
For each issue:
1. Read the sentence first
2. Decide if the suggestion matches your meaning
3. Click Change (or Ignore if it is correct)

Recommended corrections in this practice text:
- Microsft -> Microsoft
- documants -> documents
- ribon -> ribbon
- creat -> create
- printt -> print
- mistaks -> mistakes
- chekc -> check
- grammer -> grammar
- carefull -> careful
- sugestions -> suggestions
- especialy -> especially
- tecnical -> technical

You only need to fix 10, but try to fix all.
Beginner rule:
Do not click Change All unless you checked the word in every use.

Step 4: Re-run the check
After finishing, run F7 again to confirm the document is clean.
Expected result:
Word should say spelling and grammar check is complete.

Common beginner problems (quick fixes)
"Word wants to change a correct name."
Fix:
Choose Ignore, or Add to Dictionary if you will use it often.
"Word keeps stopping on the same word."
Fix:
You may be choosing Ignore Once instead of Ignore All.
"Word suggests a change that feels wrong."
Fix:
Ignore it. Trust your meaning.

Quick check (self-test)
- What does red underline mean?
- What does green underline mean?
- When should you use Add to Dictionary?
- Why should you double-check grammar suggestions?

CHAPTER 2: COMMENTS FOR FEEDBACK

Comments are notes you attach to specific words or sentences without changing the main text. They are useful for feedback, revision reminders, and teamwork.

This chapter covers:
- adding comments
- editing and deleting comments
- replying to comments (Word 2007 method)
- printing with or without comments
- a practice task: comment on 3 sentences for revision notes

1) What Comments Are Used For

Use comments to:
- suggest improvements without rewriting the text
- ask questions (example: "Can you clarify this point?")
- mark sections to revisit later
- leave feedback for someone else

Beginner rule:
Use comments for notes. Use Track Changes for actual editing (next chapter).

2) How to Add a Comment (Word 2007)

1. Select the word or sentence you want to comment on
2. Click the **Review** tab
3. Click **New Comment**
4. Type your comment in the balloon on the right side

Shortcut method:
- Select text, then press **Ctrl + Alt + M** (if supported on your keyboard setup)

Beginner tip:
Comment on a short selection. Do not select a whole page.

3) Edit, Delete, and Move Between Comments

Edit a comment
- Click inside the comment text and type changes

Delete a comment
1. Click the comment balloon
2. Review tab > Delete

Move between comments

- Review tab > Previous / Next (in the Comments group)

Beginner rule:
If you delete the selected text in the document, the comment can also disappear. Keep comments attached to stable text like a sentence, not a single word that you might delete.

4) Replying to Comments in Word 2007

Word 2007 does not have a modern "Reply" button like newer versions. The beginner method is:
Option A: Add a new comment next to the original comment
1. Click near the same sentence
2. Insert another comment
3. Start your reply with:
   Reply: ...

Option B: Add your reply inside the same comment
1. Click inside the comment
2. Press Enter
3. Type:
   Reply: ...

Beginner rule:
Keep replies short so the document stays readable.

5) Printing With Comments (Or Without)

Comments can be printed, but most final documents should be printed without them.

To print without comments (clean copy)
1. Click **Office Button**
2. Click **Print**
3. Choose print options and print normally
   If comments still print, adjust the print setting:
- In Print dialog, look for "Print what" or "Document" options
- Choose **Document** (not Document showing markup)

To print with comments (for review)
1. Review tab
2. In Tracking group, choose **Final Showing Markup**
3. Office Button > Print
4. Print the document for review

Beginner note:
If you do not see comments on print preview, check that markup is enabled.

Practice Example (15 to 20 minutes)
Goal: Comment on 3 sentences for revision notes.
Step 1: Type a short paragraph
Open a new document and type this:
Microsoft Word helps beginners create clean documents. Good formatting improves readability. A document should be reviewed before printing and sharing.
Step 2: Add comment 1 (clarity)
　　1. Select the first sentence
　　2. Review tab > New Comment
　　3. Type:
　　　　Add one example of a clean document, like a letter or report.
Step 3: Add comment 2 (formatting reminder)
　　1. Select the second sentence
　　2. New Comment
　　3. Type:
　　　　Mention fonts, spacing, and headings as simple formatting examples.
Step 4: Add comment 3 (review reminder)
　　1. Select the third sentence
　　2. New Comment
　　3. Type:
　　　　Add a note about using Spelling & Grammar before printing.
Expected result:
You now have 3 comments attached to 3 sentences.
Step 5: Navigate between comments
　　1. Review tab
　　2. Click Next to move through comments
　　3. Click Previous to go back
Optional:
Delete one comment and confirm it disappears.

Common beginner problems (quick fixes)
"I cannot see comments."

Fix:
- Review tab > Show Markup > ensure Comments is checked
- View tab > Print Layout is often easier to see comments

"My comment is attached to the wrong text."
Fix:
- Delete the comment
- Select the correct text
- Add it again

"Comments are printing and I do not want them."
Fix:
Print the clean document, not the markup version:
- set display to Final (not Final Showing Markup) before printing

Quick check (self-test)
- What is the purpose of comments?
- Where do you add a new comment?
- How do you "reply" to a comment in Word 2007?
- When should you print with comments?

CHAPTER 3: TRACK CHANGES FOR EDITING

Track Changes is the safest way to edit a document when:
- you want to see exactly what was changed
- you want someone else to review your edits
- you want to accept or reject edits one by one
- you want to avoid losing the original text

This chapter covers:
- turning Track Changes on and off
- making edits while tracking
- viewing changes clearly
- accepting and rejecting changes
- a practice task: edit a paragraph, then accept all changes

1) What Track Changes Does

When Track Changes is ON:
- deletions appear marked (often with strikethrough or balloons)
- insertions appear highlighted
- formatting changes can also be tracked

Beginner rule:
If you are editing someone else's document, use Track Changes instead of rewriting silently.

2) Turn Track Changes On and Off (Word 2007)

Turn ON
1. Click the **Review** tab
2. Click **Track Changes** (it becomes active)

Now any typing, deleting, or formatting changes will be recorded.

Turn OFF
- Click Track Changes again to toggle it off

Beginner warning:
Turning Track Changes off does not remove tracked edits. It only stops tracking new edits.

3) Viewing Changes (Final vs Original)

Word can display changes in different views.
In Word 2007, you often see options like:
- Final Showing Markup

- Final
- Original Showing Markup
- Original

Where:
- Review tab > Tracking group (Display for Review)

Beginner rule:
To review edits clearly, use "Final Showing Markup."
To read the clean version, use "Final."

4) Accept or Reject Changes
You can accept or reject changes one by one, or all at once.

Accept one change
1. Click on a tracked change
2. Review tab > Accept
3. Word keeps the change and moves to the next (depending on your settings)

Reject one change
1. Click on a tracked change
2. Review tab > Reject

Accept all changes
1. Review tab
2. Click the small drop-down under **Accept**
3. Choose **Accept All Changes in Document**

Beginner rule:
Do not accept all until you quickly review the document first.

5) Show or Hide Markup (What You See)
Sometimes markup makes the page look messy. You can control what is shown.

Common controls:
- Review tab > Show Markup
- Choose what you want to see:
    - Comments
    - Insertions and Deletions
    - Formatting

Beginner tip:
If you only want to review text edits, turn off Formatting in Show Markup.

Practice Example (20 to 25 minutes)

Goal: Edit a paragraph with Track Changes, then accept all.

Step 1: Type a practice paragraph

Open a new document and type this:

Microsoft Word helps beginners write documents quickly. It is easy to make mistakes when typing fast. Editing is important because it improves clarity and reduces errors.

Step 2: Turn on Track Changes

1. Review tab
2. Click **Track Changes**

Step 3: Make edits (while Track Changes is ON)

Edit the paragraph like this (your edits will show as tracked):

- Change "quickly" to "clearly"
- Replace "It is easy to make mistakes when typing fast" with:
  "When you type fast, mistakes are common."
- Add one extra sentence at the end:
  "Always review your work before printing."

You should now see visible tracked edits.

Step 4: View changes clearly

1. Review tab
2. In Tracking, set Display to **Final Showing Markup**
3. Scroll through and confirm you can see insertions and deletions

Step 5: Accept all changes

1. Review tab
2. Click the drop-down under **Accept**
3. Choose **Accept All Changes in Document**

Step 6: Turn Track Changes off (so future typing is normal)

- Review tab > Track Changes (toggle OFF)

Expected result:

- your paragraph now shows the final version without markup
- your edits remain, but the tracking marks are gone

Common beginner problems (quick fixes)

"I turned off Track Changes but I still see markup."

Fix:

You turned tracking off, but you did not accept or reject the

changes.
Accept or reject changes to remove markup.
"I cannot see the edits."
Fix:
Set display to Final Showing Markup.
"My page looks too messy."
Fix:
Use Show Markup to hide Formatting or Comments temporarily.

Quick check (self-test)
- What does Track Changes do?
- Where do you turn Track Changes on and off?
- What is the difference between Final and Final Showing Markup?
- How do you accept all changes in the document?

CHAPTER 4: COMPARE AND COMBINE DOCUMENTS

When you have two versions of the same document, Word 2007 can:
- compare them to show what changed
- combine edits into one document (useful for teamwork)

This chapter covers:
- what Compare does
- what Combine does
- how to compare two versions
- how to merge edits safely
- a practice task: compare two versions of the same file

1) Compare vs Combine (Simple Difference)

Compare

Compare shows differences between:
- the original document
  and
- a revised document

Result:
Word creates a new document that shows changes (like Track Changes), so you can review what was added, deleted, or edited.

Combine

Combine merges edits from:
- two documents that both have tracked changes

Result:
Word creates a new document that contains both sets of edits, so you can accept or reject them.

Beginner rule:
If you only want to see what changed, use Compare.
If you want to merge edits from two editors, use Combine.

2) What You Need Before Comparing Documents

For a clean compare, you should have:
- Version 1 (Original)
- Version 2 (Revised)

Beginner rule:
Save versions with clear names, for example:
- Report_v1.docx

- Report_v2.docx

3) How to Compare Two Documents (Word 2007)
1. Click the **Review** tab
2. In the Compare group, click **Compare**
3. Choose **Compare…**
4. Under Original document:
- browse and select Version 1
5. Under Revised document:
- browse and select Version 2
6. Click **OK**

Word creates a new document showing differences with markup.

Beginner tip:
Do not edit inside the compare result until you understand what you are seeing. Treat it as a review copy.

4) How to Combine Documents (Basic Use)
Use Combine when two people edited separate copies with Track Changes.

Steps:
1. Review tab > Compare
2. Choose **Combine…**
3. Select:
- Original document
- Revised document (first editor)
4. Click OK
   Then repeat Combine again if you have a third editor copy.

Beginner rule:
Combine is for teamwork and tracked edits. If Track Changes was not used, Compare is usually enough.

5) How to Read the Compare Result
In the compare output you may see:
- insertions highlighted
- deletions marked
- formatting changes indicated
- comments shown (if present)

Use:

- Next / Previous (Review tab) to jump through changes
- Accept / Reject to finalize changes if you want to create a final version

Beginner tip:
Change the view to Final Showing Markup to see everything, then switch to Final to read cleanly.

Practice Example (25 to 35 minutes)
Goal: Compare two versions of the same file.
Step 1: Create Version 1 (Original)
1. Open a new document
2. Type this paragraph:

This report explains basic Word 2007 skills for beginners. It includes typing, formatting, and printing. The goal is to help new users work confidently.

3. Save it as:
   Report_v1.docx

Step 2: Create Version 2 (Revised)
1. Click Office Button > Save As
2. Save a new copy as:
   Report_v2.docx

Now edit the text in Report_v2.docx like this:
- Change "basic" to "essential"
- Add one new sentence:
  "These skills also help students prepare academic assignments."
- Remove the word "confidently" and replace it with "with fewer mistakes"

Save Report_v2.docx.

Step 3: Compare the two versions
1. Open Word (you can be in either file or a new blank document)
2. Review tab
3. Compare > Compare...
4. Original: choose Report_v1.docx
5. Revised: choose Report_v2.docx
6. OK

Expected result:
A new document appears showing the differences.

Step 4: Review changes
1. Use Review tab > Next to move through each change
2. Switch display:
- Final Showing Markup (to see changes)
- Final (to read cleanly)

Optional:
Accept all changes to create a final document:
- Accept drop-down > Accept All Changes in Document

Common beginner problems (quick fixes)
"Compare is greyed out."
Fix:
Make sure you are not in a restricted view or protected document. Also confirm you opened Word normally and the document is editable.

"Nothing shows as changed."
Fix:
You may have compared the same file twice. Check that you selected v1 as Original and v2 as Revised.

"The result is confusing."
Fix:
Use Next/Previous to view changes one at a time, and hide formatting markup if it is distracting:
- Show Markup > uncheck Formatting

Quick check (self-test)
- What is the purpose of Compare?
- What is the purpose of Combine?
- Where do you find Compare in Word 2007?
- Why should you save clear version names like v1 and v2?

CHAPTER 5: PROTECTING A DOCUMENT

Protecting a document helps you control what other people can change. In Word 2007 you can:
- restrict formatting
- restrict editing (read-only, comments only, tracked changes only, form filling)
- add a password (with important warnings)

This chapter covers:
- basic protection options
- safe beginner advice
- a practice task: restrict formatting and editing for a shared document

1) Why Protect a Document

Protection is useful when:
- you share a template and want others to fill in only certain parts
- you want reviewers to comment without rewriting
- you want edits to be tracked
- you want formatting to stay consistent

Beginner rule:
Protection is for control, not for hiding information. Do not treat it like strong security.

2) What "Restrict Formatting" Means

Restrict formatting means:
- people cannot freely change fonts, spacing, styles
- they are limited to approved styles (if you set it up)

Good for:
- forms
- templates
- official letters and reports where design must stay consistent

3) What "Restrict Editing" Means

Restrict editing controls what people can do:
- No changes (Read only)
- Comments
- Tracked changes

- Filling in forms

Good for:
- feedback review (comments only)
- controlled collaboration (tracked changes only)
- simple forms (filling in forms)

Beginner rule:
If you want someone to edit but not hide edits, choose "Tracked changes."

4) Password Warnings (Very Important)
Word 2007 can set passwords for:
- opening a file
- modifying a file
- removing protection

Beginner warnings:
- if you forget the password, you can lose access
- passwords can be weak if shared or guessed
- do not rely on passwords as your only security for sensitive documents

Beginner rule:
Write passwords down in a safe place. Use protection mainly to prevent accidental changes.

5) Where Document Protection Is Found (Word 2007)
1. Click the **Review** tab
2. Look for **Protect Document** (or "Protect Document" button in the Protect group)

From there you can open:
- Restrict Formatting and Editing

Practice Example (20 to 25 minutes)
Goal: Restrict formatting and editing for a shared document.
Step 1: Create a short shared document
Open a new Word document and type:
Shared Document Template
Name: _____
Date: _____
Topic: _____
Instructions:
Please fill in the blanks. Do not change the formatting.

Save it as:
Shared_Template.docx

Step 2: Open Restrict Formatting and Editing
1. Review tab
2. Click **Protect Document**
3. Choose **Restrict Formatting and Editing**

A protection panel appears on the right.

Step 3: Restrict formatting
1. Under Formatting restrictions, check:
   Limit formatting to a selection of styles
2. Click **Settings**
3. For beginner practice:
   - keep only a few basic styles allowed (Normal, Heading 1, Heading 2)
4. Click OK

Beginner tip:
If you are unsure, leave more styles allowed. Too few styles can frustrate users.

Step 4: Restrict editing
1. Under Editing restrictions, check:
   Allow only this type of editing in the document
2. From the drop-down, choose:
   No changes (Read only)

Optional (better for review):
Choose:
Tracked changes
This allows editing but keeps a record.

Step 5: Start enforcement (apply protection)
1. Click:
   Yes, Start Enforcing Protection
2. Enter a password (optional for practice)
   If you use one, write it down.
3. Click OK

Expected result:
- formatting changes become limited
- editing becomes restricted based on your choice

Step 6: Test the restrictions
Try to:
- change the font
- delete headings

- type in random areas

You should see restrictions working.

Step 7: Stop protection (to edit again)
1. Review tab > Protect Document
2. Restrict Formatting and Editing
3. Click **Stop Protection**
4. Enter password if required

Common beginner problems (quick fixes)
"I cannot edit my own document now."
Fix:
Stop protection from the Restrict panel. Use the password if you set one.
"Users cannot fill in the blanks."
Fix:
Read-only blocks all editing. If the document is meant to be filled:
- use "Filling in forms" and form controls, or
- leave editing allowed but restrict formatting only

"Too many styles are blocked."
Fix:
Adjust the allowed styles list in Formatting restrictions settings.

Quick check (self-test)
- What is the difference between restricting formatting and restricting editing?
- Which editing mode is best when you want people to edit but keep a record?
- Why should you be careful with passwords?
- Where do you turn protection on and off in Word 2007?

PART X: VIEW AND NAVIGATION (VIEW TAB)
CHAPTER 1: VIEWS EXPLAINED

Word 2007 has different views so you can work in the way that matches your task. Some views help with reading, some help with editing, and some help with organizing long documents. This chapter covers:
- Print Layout
- Draft
- Web Layout
- Outline
- Reading view
- a practice task: switch views and explain what changed

1) Where Views Are Found
Go to:
- **View** tab

Look for:
- Document Views group

You can also switch views using the small view buttons near the bottom-right of the Word window (depending on your setup).

2) Print Layout View (Most Common)
What it is

Print Layout shows your document as it will look when printed.

Best for
- formatting and layout (margins, headers, footers, page numbers)
- working with images, tables, and page breaks
- final checks before printing

What you see clearly
- page boundaries
- headers and footers
- page breaks
- margins and spacing

Beginner rule:
Use Print Layout for most normal work.

3) Draft View (Fast Editing)
What it is

Draft view simplifies the page display so Word can focus on text.

Best for
- fast typing and editing
- long documents where Print Layout feels slow
- focusing on words instead of layout

What you do not see well
- headers and footers
- precise page layout
- some objects may appear differently

Beginner rule:
Use Draft when you only want to write and edit quickly.

4) Web Layout View (Looks Like a Web Page)
What it is

Web Layout shows the document like it would appear on a web page (continuous flow).

Best for
- documents meant to be read on screen
- checking how content flows without pages

What changes
- pages disappear (continuous scrolling)
- objects may shift to fit the screen width

Beginner rule:
Use Web Layout only if you are writing for online reading.

5) Outline View (Best for Structure)
What it is

Outline view helps you work with headings and document structure.

Best for
- organizing long documents
- moving whole sections up and down
- checking Heading levels (Heading 1, Heading 2, etc.)

What changes
- you can collapse and expand headings
- body text can be shown or hidden under headings

- you can reorder sections quickly

Beginner rule:
If your document is long and confusing, Outline view can save you.

6) Reading View (Comfortable Reading)
What it is
Reading view is designed to make reading easier and reduce editing distractions.
Best for
- reading and reviewing
- checking flow and clarity
- viewing comments and markup in a reader-friendly way

What changes
- editing tools are limited
- the layout looks more like a book reader

Beginner rule:
Use Reading view to review, not to format.

Practice Example (15 to 20 minutes)
Goal: Switch views and explain what changed.
Step 1: Create a simple mixed document
Open a new Word document and type:
Views Practice
Introduction
This document is used to practice Word views.
Add a table:
- Insert tab > Table > 2 columns and 2 rows
  Type:
  Item | Notes
  View | Changes how you see the document

Add a page break:
- Press Ctrl + Enter

Type:
Second Page
This page helps you notice page boundaries in Print Layout.

Step 2: Switch to Print Layout
1. View tab
2. Click **Print Layout**

What to notice:
- you see real pages
- you can clearly see the page break
- margins and spacing are visible

Explain (say out loud or write a short note):
Print Layout shows how it will print.

Step 3: Switch to Draft
1. View tab
2. Click **Draft**

What to notice:
- pages feel less strict
- layout details are reduced
- focus is on text

Explain:
Draft is best for fast writing and editing.

Step 4: Switch to Web Layout
1. View tab
2. Click **Web Layout**

What to notice:
- pages disappear into a continuous scroll
- the content flows like a web page

Explain:
Web Layout is best for screen reading and web-style flow.

Step 5: Switch to Outline
1. View tab
2. Click **Outline**

What to notice:
- headings become the main structure
- you can expand or collapse sections
- you can move sections (if headings are styled)

Explain:
Outline helps organize long documents by headings.

Step 6: Switch to Reading View
1. View tab
2. Click **Full Screen Reading** (or Reading view option)

What to notice:
- the page is optimized for reading
- editing options are limited

Explain:
Reading view is best for reviewing and reading, not heavy editing.
Step 7: Return to Print Layout
Switch back to Print Layout to finish.

Common beginner problems (quick fixes)
"Outline view looks useless."
Fix:
Apply Heading styles to your headings first. Outline works best with real Heading 1 and Heading 2 styles.
"I cannot edit much in Reading view."
Fix:
Exit Reading view and return to Print Layout or Draft for editing.
"My table looks different in Web Layout."
Fix:
That is normal. Web Layout adjusts content to screen width.

Quick check (self-test)
- Which view is best for printing and page setup?
- Which view is best for fast typing?
- Which view helps you reorder sections using headings?
- Which view is best for reading only?

CHAPTER 2: ZOOM, SPLIT, AND SIDE-BY-SIDE READING

Word 2007 includes view tools that make reading and reviewing easier, especially for long documents. These tools do not change your content. They only change how you see it on screen.

This chapter covers:
- Zoom tools
- Split window
- View Side by Side
- useful reading habits
- a practice task: split the window and compare two pages

1) Zoom (Make Text Comfortable)

Zoom changes the size of what you see on screen. It does not change font size in the document.

Where Zoom is found
- View tab > Zoom group
  Common options:
- Zoom (opens a dialog)
- 100%
- One Page
- Two Pages
- Page Width

When to use each option
- 100%: normal working size
- Page Width: best for reading without side scrolling
- One Page: good for checking overall layout
- Two Pages: good for reviewing page flow, like a book

Beginner rule:
Use Page Width for comfortable reading. Use 100% for editing.

2) Split (Two Parts of the Same Document)

Split divides your window into two panes so you can view two parts of the same document at once.

Use Split when:
- you want to compare page 1 and page 3

- you want to copy a paragraph from one section to another
- you want to check headings while writing later pages

Where:
- View tab > Split

How it works:
- top pane and bottom pane show the same document
- you can scroll each pane independently

Beginner rule:
Split is for one document. Side by Side is for two documents.

3) View Side by Side (Two Different Documents)

View Side by Side lets you see two separate documents next to each other.

Use it when:
- you are comparing two versions (v1 and v2)
- you are copying content from one file to another
- you are checking a reference document while writing

Where:
- View tab > View Side by Side
  Often used together with:
- Synchronous Scrolling (scroll both at once)

Beginner rule:
Side by Side is best for comparing two files.

4) Useful Comfort Reading Habits

Simple habits that help beginners:
- use Page Width zoom for reading
- switch to Full Screen Reading for long reading
- use Split to keep your introduction visible while writing later pages
- use Two Pages zoom to check how pages look together

Practice Example (15 to 25 minutes)

Goal: Split the window and compare two pages in the same document.

Step 1: Create a two-page document
Open a new Word document and type:
Split Practice

Page 1 content:
This is the first page. It includes an introduction and a short paragraph.
Now press:
Ctrl + Enter
(to insert a page break)
Page 2 content:
This is the second page. It includes a second paragraph and a short conclusion.
Save the file as:
Split Practice.docx

Step 2: Turn on Split
1. Click the **View** tab
2. Click **Split**

A horizontal split bar appears, creating:
- top pane
- bottom pane

Step 3: Show page 1 in the top pane
1. Click inside the top pane
2. Scroll to Page 1
3. Keep it there

Step 4: Show page 2 in the bottom pane
1. Click inside the bottom pane
2. Scroll to Page 2
3. Keep it there

Now you can compare both pages at the same time.

Step 5: Adjust the split size
- Drag the split bar up or down to give more space to one pane.

Step 6: Remove Split
1. View tab
2. Click **Remove Split**
   Or double-click the split bar.

Expected result:
Your document returns to a normal single view.

Optional mini-practice: Zoom for comfort
Try these quickly:
- View > Zoom > Page Width (comfortable reading)
- View > Two Pages (book-style review)

- Return to 100% for editing

Common beginner problems (quick fixes)
"Split is greyed out."
Fix:
Switch to Print Layout first:
- View tab > Print Layout
  Then try Split again.

"Both panes scroll together."
Fix:
Click inside one pane and scroll. They should scroll independently. If you used another tool like synchronous scrolling with side-by-side documents, turn that off.

"I cannot tell which pane I am editing."
Fix:
Click inside the pane you want. The cursor shows where you are typing.

Quick check (self-test)
- Does Zoom change your document font size?
- What is the difference between Split and View Side by Side?
- When is Page Width zoom useful?
- How do you remove the split?

CHAPTER 3: SHOW/HIDE MARKS TO FIX MESSY DOCUMENTS

Messy documents usually look fine at first, but they behave badly when you format or print. Show/Hide marks reveal what is really inside your document: extra spaces, hidden paragraph marks, tabs, and breaks. Once you can see them, you can fix problems fast.

This chapter covers:
- what Show/Hide marks are
- what each mark means
- how to fix common messes
- a practice task: remove double spaces and extra blank lines

1) What Show/Hide Marks Are

Show/Hide displays formatting marks that are normally hidden, such as:
- paragraph marks (¶)
- spaces (·)
- tabs (→)
- line breaks
- page breaks and section breaks

Beginner rule:
If your document spacing looks weird, turn on Show/Hide.

2) Where to Turn On Show/Hide

Most common location:
- **Home tab** > Paragraph group > **Show/Hide** (¶)

You can also use it while working on layout and cleanup.

3) What the Marks Mean (Beginner Guide)

Paragraph mark (¶)
Appears when you press Enter.
- One paragraph mark = one paragraph.

Common beginner mistake:
Using many Enter presses to create spacing. This creates many ¶ marks and causes layout problems.

Space dot (·)
Appears between words when you press the Spacebar.
Common beginner mistake:
Using multiple spaces to align text. This breaks alignment later.

Tab arrow (→)
Appears when you press Tab.
Tabs are good for:
- moving to a specific position
- aligning text quickly (but tables are better for full alignment)

Page break line
Appears when you press Ctrl + Enter.
A page break is correct when you want:
- a new page that stays a new page even if you add text earlier.

Section break
Used for:
- different headers/footers
- different page numbering
- switching orientation in part of a document

Beginner rule:
Do not use section breaks unless you truly need them.

4) Fixing Messy Documents (Most Common Problems)

Problem A: Double spaces between words
Fix:
Use Find and Replace.
- Find: two spaces
- Replace: one space

Problem B: Extra blank lines
Fix:
Delete extra paragraph marks, or use Find and Replace:
- Find: ¶¶
- Replace: ¶

Repeat until clean.

Problem C: Manual alignment using spaces
Fix:
Remove extra spaces and use:
- tabs, or
- tables, or
- paragraph indentation settings

Beginner rule:
Never align columns using spaces.

Practice Example (20 to 25 minutes)
Goal: Fix double spaces and extra blank lines.
Step 1: Create a messy practice text
Open a new document and type this exactly:
This is a messy document.
It has double spaces between words.
It also has extra blank lines.
The goal is to clean it up fast.
Notice:
- double spaces in many places
- extra blank lines between paragraphs

Step 2: Turn on Show/Hide
1. Home tab
2. Click **Show/Hide** (¶)

What you will see:
- dots between words (spaces)
- paragraph marks at the end of lines
- multiple paragraph marks where blank lines exist

Step 3: Fix double spaces using Replace
1. Press **Ctrl + H** (Find and Replace)
2. In Find what, type:
   (two spaces)
3. In Replace with, type:
   (one space)
4. Click **Replace All**

Important:
Do this again if needed, because triple spaces become double spaces after the first replace.
Beginner rule:
Repeat Replace All until Word says it found 0 matches.

Step 4: Fix extra blank lines
You can do it manually or with Replace.

Quick Replace method
1. Press Ctrl + H
2. In Find what, type:
   ^p^p
   (This means two paragraph marks)
3. In Replace with, type:
   ^p
4. Click Replace All

Repeat until the document has normal spacing.
Beginner tip:
Do not remove all blank lines if you want a space between paragraphs. You want one blank line or one spacing standard, not none.

Step 5: Keep Show/Hide on while checking
Scan your document:
- only one space dot between words
- only one paragraph mark between paragraphs (unless you want a blank line)

Then turn Show/Hide off when finished.

Common beginner problems (quick fixes)
"I deleted a blank line but spacing still looks too large."
Fix:
Check paragraph spacing (Before/After) in paragraph settings. Extra space can be paragraph spacing, not blank lines.

"Replace removed spacing I wanted."
Fix:
Undo (Ctrl + Z), then replace carefully. Do not replace all paragraph marks.

"I still see odd gaps."
Fix:
Show/Hide may reveal tabs, manual line breaks, or section breaks causing the issue.

Quick check (self-test)
- What does the paragraph mark (¶) represent?
- What does the dot (·) represent?
- What shortcut opens Find and Replace?
- What is the safest way to remove double spaces across a document?

PART XI: THE HIDDEN TOOLS (CONTEXTUAL TABS)
CHAPTER 1: WHAT CONTEXTUAL TABS ARE

In Word 2007, some tools are "hidden" until you click a specific object. These are called Contextual Tabs. They appear only when you select something that needs special tools, like a picture, a table, a chart, or SmartArt.

This chapter covers:
- what contextual tabs are
- why they only appear sometimes
- common examples (Picture Tools, Table Tools, Drawing Tools)
- a practice task: click a picture and find Picture Tools

1) What Contextual Tabs Are (Simple Meaning)
A contextual tab is a special tab on the Ribbon that appears only when it is relevant.
Example:
- If you click a picture, Word shows **Picture Tools**
- If you click a table, Word shows **Table Tools**
- If you click a chart, Word shows **Chart Tools**

Beginner rule:
If you cannot find a tool, click the object first.

2) Why Contextual Tabs Appear Only Sometimes
They appear only when Word detects you selected an object that needs extra commands.
Reason:
It keeps the Ribbon simpler and avoids showing tools you do not need.
What triggers them:
- selecting an image
- selecting a table
- selecting a shape or text box
- selecting SmartArt
- selecting a chart

What makes them disappear:
- clicking outside the object
- clicking normal text

3) Common Contextual Tabs in Word 2007
Picture Tools
Appears when you select a picture.
Used for:
- resizing
- cropping
- text wrapping
- position and alignment
- picture styles

Table Tools
Appears when you select a table.
Used for:
- inserting rows and columns
- table styles
- borders and shading
- layout settings

Drawing Tools
Appears when you select a shape, text box, or WordArt.
Used for:
- fill color
- outline
- effects
- alignment
- grouping

Chart Tools
Appears when you select a chart.
Used for:
- changing chart type
- formatting chart elements
- editing data

Beginner tip:
Contextual tabs often have two sub-tabs, like Design and Layout (depending on the object).

Practice Example (10 to 15 minutes)
Goal: Click a picture and find Picture Tools.
Step 1: Insert a picture
1. Open a new Word document
2. Click the **Insert** tab

3. Click **Picture**
4. Choose any image file on your computer
5. Click Insert

The picture appears in the document.

Step 2: Click the picture
1. Click once on the picture

Expected result:

A new tab area appears on the Ribbon:
- **Picture Tools**

Often you will see a sub-tab like:
- Format

Step 3: Identify what changed

Look for:
- a new Picture Tools tab (or Picture Tools > Format)
- picture editing tools such as:
  - Crop
  - Size
  - Wrap Text
  - Position
  - Picture Styles

Step 4: Make one safe change (optional)

Try:
- Wrap Text > Square
  Then click outside the picture to see Picture Tools disappear.

Common beginner problems (quick fixes)

"I do not see Picture Tools."

Fix:

Make sure the picture is selected. Click directly on the image until you see selection handles around it.

"Picture Tools disappears when I try to click it."

Fix:

You clicked outside the picture. Click the picture again, then go to Picture Tools.

"I inserted the picture but cannot move it."

Fix:

Change text wrapping:
- Picture Tools > Wrap Text > Square or Tight

Quick check (self-test)
- What are contextual tabs?
- Why do they appear only sometimes?
- What must you do to make Picture Tools appear?
- Name two other objects that trigger contextual tabs.

CHAPTER 2: TABLE TOOLS (DESIGN AND LAYOUT)

Tables are one of the fastest ways to make information clear. In Word 2007, table tools are hidden until you click inside a table. When you do, Word shows **Table Tools** with two main tabs:

- Design
- Layout

This chapter covers:
- how to open Table Tools
- borders and shading
- alignment and spacing
- simple sorting basics
- a practice task: format a table to look clean and readable

1) How to Show Table Tools
1. Click anywhere inside a table
2. Look at the Ribbon
3. You will see **Table Tools** appear
4. Under it, you will see:

- **Design**
- **Layout**

Beginner rule:
If you cannot find table formatting tools, click inside the table first.

2) Table Tools Design Tab (How the Table Looks)
The Design tab is mainly for appearance.
Table Styles (fast clean look)
- Choose a built-in style to instantly format the table.

Beginner tip:
Choose a simple style with light shading. Avoid heavy colors unless required.

Borders
Borders control the lines around cells.
Common beginner uses:
- show all borders (for clear grids)
- remove inside borders (for a cleaner look)
- keep only top and bottom borders (common in reports)

Shading
Shading fills cells with a color.
Best practice:
- shade the header row lightly
- keep the rest white for readability

Beginner rule:
Use light shading. Dark shading makes text hard to read.

3) Table Tools Layout Tab (How the Table Works)
The Layout tab is mainly for structure and alignment.
Alignment
Align text inside cells:
- top, middle, bottom
- left, center, right

Best practice:
- header row centered or left aligned
- numbers usually right aligned
- normal text usually left aligned

Cell size
- adjust row height and column width
- use AutoFit to fit content or window

Merge and split cells
- merge cells for a single heading across columns
- split cells when you need more columns

Sort (basic)
Sort helps organize table rows, for example:
- sort by Name (A to Z)
- sort by Date
- sort by City

Beginner warning:
Sorting changes the order of rows. Make sure your table has a clear header row first.

Practice Example (20 to 30 minutes)
Goal: Format a table to look clean and readable.
Step 1: Create a simple table
Open a new document and insert a table:
- Insert tab > Table > 4 columns and 6 rows

Fill it like this:

Name | City | Category | Phone
John Deng | Juba | Member | 0920 000 001
Mary Ajak | Bor | Donor | 0920 000 002
Peter James | Yei | Member | 0920 000 003
Sarah Lado | Juba | Staff | 0920 000 004
David Gai | Nimule | Donor | 0920 000 005

Step 2: Open Table Tools

Click inside the table to show:
- Table Tools > Design and Layout

Step 3: Make the header row stand out

1. Click the first row (header row)
2. Table Tools > Design
3. Apply:
- a light shading color, or choose a table style that includes a header row design
4. Make header text bold:
- Home tab > Bold

Beginner tip:
If you apply a table style, you may not need manual shading.

Step 4: Clean borders

1. Click inside the table
2. Table Tools > Design > Borders
3. Choose a clean option:
- All Borders (clear grid), or
- Outside Borders + Inside Horizontal Borders (cleaner look)

Beginner rule:
Avoid random border choices. Keep it consistent.

Step 5: Align text properly

1. Select the whole table (click the table move handle at top-left of the table)
2. Table Tools > Layout > Alignment
3. Choose:
- middle left (often best for readability)

Now fix specific columns:
- Phone column: align center or right
- Category column: center can look clean

Step 6: Adjust column widths

1. Click inside the table
2. Table Tools > Layout

3. Use AutoFit:
   - AutoFit to Contents (if text is tight), or
   - AutoFit to Window (if you want it to stretch neatly)

Beginner tip:
AutoFit to Window is great for readability when printing.

Step 7: Sort the table (basic)
Sort by City:
1. Click inside the table
2. Table Tools > Layout > Sort
3. Sort by:
   City
4. Type:
   Text
5. Order:
   Ascending
6. Check:
   My list has header row
7. OK

Expected result:
Rows are re-ordered by City alphabetically, while each row stays intact.

What a "Clean Table" Looks Like (Checklist)
A clean table usually has:
- clear header row (bold, light shading)
- consistent borders
- readable alignment
- enough spacing (not cramped)
- columns sized to fit content

Common beginner problems (quick fixes)
"My table looks messy after formatting."
Fix:
Undo (Ctrl + Z) and apply one simple Table Style instead of many manual changes.

"Sorting mixed up my data."
Fix:
Undo immediately (Ctrl + Z). Then sort again and ensure: "My list has header row" is checked.

"Text looks cramped."

Fix:
AutoFit to Window, and reduce font size slightly if needed.

Quick check (self-test)
- How do you make Table Tools appear?
- Which tab controls the look: Design or Layout?
- Which tab controls alignment and sorting?
- What is one safe way to make a table readable fast?

CHAPTER 3: PICTURE TOOLS (FORMAT)

Pictures can make a document clearer, but beginners often struggle with moving, cropping, and aligning them. Picture Tools in Word 2007 give you the controls you need, but they appear only when you click the picture.

This chapter covers:
- how to open Picture Tools
- cropping
- corrections (basic)
- size and position
- wrap text (the key to control)
- a practice task: crop a picture and align it with text

1) How to Show Picture Tools
1. Click the picture once
2. Look at the Ribbon
3. You will see **Picture Tools**
4. Click the **Format** tab under Picture Tools

Beginner rule:
No Picture Tools visible means the picture is not selected.

2) Wrap Text (The Most Important Picture Skill)
Wrap Text controls how text flows around the picture.
Common wrap options:
- In Line with Text (acts like a big letter, hard to position)
- Square (best for most beginners)
- Tight (similar to Square but closer)
- Top and Bottom (text above and below only)
- Behind Text (can be confusing)
- In Front of Text (can be confusing)

Beginner rule:
Use Square for most documents. It gives you control without chaos.

How to set it:
1. Click the picture
2. Picture Tools > Format
3. Click **Text Wrapping**
4. Choose **Square**

3) Crop (Remove Unwanted Parts)
Cropping cuts away parts of the picture without deleting the file.

How to crop:
1. Click the picture
2. Picture Tools > Format
3. Click **Crop**
4. Black crop handles appear around the picture
5. Drag handles inward to remove unwanted areas
6. Press Enter or click outside the picture to finish

Beginner tip:
If you crop too much, you can crop again and pull the handles back outward.

4) Corrections (Basic)
Word 2007 has basic picture adjustments. Depending on your Word 2007 setup, you may see:
- brightness and contrast tools
- recolor options
- compress pictures

Beginner rule:
Do not over-edit pictures in Word. Keep it simple. If a picture needs heavy editing, do it in an image editor first.

5) Size and Alignment
Resize correctly
- Use corner handles to resize (keeps proportions)
- Avoid side handles (can stretch and distort)

Align with text
Use alignment tools:
1. Click the picture
2. Picture Tools > Format
3. Use:
- Position
- Align
- Arrange tools

Beginner tip:
If you cannot move the picture freely, change Wrap Text away from "In Line with Text."

Practice Example (20 to 30 minutes)
Goal: Crop a picture and align it with text.
Step 1: Insert a picture
1. Open a new Word document
2. Type a short paragraph:

This document demonstrates how to insert and align a picture with text. The picture should sit neatly beside the paragraph without covering the words.

3. Press Enter once
4. Insert tab > Picture
5. Choose any photo and insert it

Step 2: Change Wrap Text to Square
1. Click the picture
2. Picture Tools > Format
3. Text Wrapping > **Square**

Now you should be able to drag the picture around.

Step 3: Crop the picture
1. Click the picture
2. Picture Tools > Format > Crop
3. Drag one side handle inward to remove an unwanted edge
4. Drag a corner handle slightly inward to tighten the frame
5. Press Enter to finish cropping

Step 4: Resize without distortion
1. Click the picture
2. Drag a corner handle inward until the picture is a reasonable size

Step 5: Align the picture neatly with text
Option A (manual alignment):
1. Drag the picture to the right side of the paragraph
2. Make sure text wraps neatly around it

Option B (Word alignment tools):
1. Click the picture
2. Picture Tools > Format
3. Align > Align Right (or Position > Top Right)

Adjust by dragging slightly if needed.
Expected result:
- picture is cropped
- picture sits beside text

- text wraps neatly and stays readable

Common beginner problems (quick fixes)
"My picture jumps to a weird location."
Fix:
Set Wrap Text to Square, then drag it into position.
"My picture looks stretched."
Fix:
Undo, then resize using corner handles only.
"Text is covering the picture."
Fix:
Use Square wrap and move the picture away from the text area. You can also set:
- Wrap Text > More Layout Options (if needed) and adjust distance from text.

Quick check (self-test)
- What must you do to see Picture Tools?
- Which wrap option is best for beginners?
- How do you crop a picture?
- Why should you resize using corner handles?

CHAPTER 4: DRAWING TOOLS FOR SHAPES AND TEXT BOXES

Shapes and text boxes help you highlight key points, create callouts, and make simple layouts. In Word 2007, the tools for shapes appear only when you select a shape or text box. These are called **Drawing Tools**.

This chapter covers:
- how to show Drawing Tools
- fill, outline, and effects
- aligning and grouping objects
- a practice task: create a simple callout box

1) How to Show Drawing Tools
1. Insert a shape or text box
2. Click the shape once to select it
3. Look at the Ribbon
4. You will see **Drawing Tools**
5. Click the **Format** tab under Drawing Tools

Beginner rule:
No Drawing Tools means the shape is not selected.

2) Fill, Outline, and Effects (The 3 Main Controls)
Shape Fill
Changes the inside color of the shape.
Good practice:
- use light fill colors for readability
- avoid very dark fills unless text is white and readable

Shape Outline
Changes the border line color and thickness.
Good practice:
- use a thin outline (1 pt or similar)
- use a neutral color (black, dark gray) for official documents

Shape Effects
Adds shadows, glow, bevel, and 3D effects.
Beginner rule:
For official documents, keep effects minimal. A light shadow is okay, but do not overdo it.

3) Text in Shapes and Text Boxes
To type inside a shape:

- click the shape, then start typing
Or:
- right-click the shape > Add Text

To format text:
- use normal text tools on the Home tab (font, size, bold)
- keep it readable (avoid fancy fonts)

Beginner tip:
Text boxes are best when you want a clean rectangle for text. Shapes are best for arrows, callouts, and labels.

4) Aligning Objects (Make It Look Neat)

Alignment helps shapes line up cleanly.
Where:
- Drawing Tools > Format > Arrange group > Align

Common align options:
- Align Left
- Align Center
- Align Right
- Align Top
- Align Middle
- Align Bottom

Beginner rule:
If you use more than one shape, align them so the document looks intentional, not random.

5) Grouping Objects (Move Them Together)

Grouping lets you combine two or more objects so they move as one.
Example:
- a rectangle shape + a text box + an arrow

How to group:
1. Hold Ctrl and click each object to select all
2. Drawing Tools > Format
3. Click **Group** > Group

To ungroup:
- Group > Ungroup

Beginner warning:
Grouping may not work if objects are "In Line with Text."
If grouping fails, set Wrap Text for each object to:

- Square

Practice Example (20 to 30 minutes)
Goal: Create a simple callout box.
A callout box is a highlighted note that draws attention.
Step 1: Type a short paragraph
Open a new Word document and type:
This chapter explains how to create callout boxes for important notes. A callout box helps the reader notice warnings and key tips.
Step 2: Insert a callout shape
1. Insert tab
2. Shapes
3. Choose a Callout shape (example: Rounded Rectangular Callout)
4. Click and drag on the page to draw it

Step 3: Add text inside the callout
Click inside the shape and type:
TIP: Use light colors and simple borders for a professional look.
Step 4: Format the callout (clean and readable)
1. Click the callout shape border to select it
2. Drawing Tools > Format

Set:
- Shape Fill: light yellow or light gray
- Shape Outline: dark gray or black
- Shape Effects: none, or a very soft shadow

Step 5: Make the text readable
1. Select the text inside the callout
2. Home tab:
- Font size: 11 or 12
- Bold the word TIP
- Keep the rest normal

Step 6: Position it neatly with text
If the shape is hard to move:
1. Click the shape
2. Drawing Tools > Format
3. Text Wrapping (or Arrange > Text Wrapping)
4. Choose **Square**

Now drag it so it sits near the paragraph without covering text.

Expected result:
- a clean callout box
- readable text inside
- positioned neatly in the document

Optional: Create a boxed note using a Text Box (even simpler)
1. Insert tab > Text Box
2. Draw a rectangle
3. Type your note
4. Format with fill and outline under Drawing Tools

Common beginner problems (quick fixes)
"I cannot move the shape freely."
Fix:
Change wrapping:
- Drawing Tools > Format > Text Wrapping > Square

"My text is too close to the border."
Fix:
Right-click shape > Format Shape > Text Box > adjust internal margins (if available)

"Grouping does not work."
Fix:
Set each object's wrap to Square, then select them with Ctrl and Group again.

Quick check (self-test)
- What makes Drawing Tools appear?
- What do Shape Fill and Shape Outline control?
- Where do you find Align tools?
- Why is Square wrapping helpful for shapes?

CHAPTER 5: HEADER AND FOOTER TOOLS

Headers and footers are the areas at the top and bottom of a page used for:
- document titles
- author name
- dates
- page numbers
- section-specific information

In Word 2007, header and footer tools appear only when you open the header or footer area. That is why many beginners think Word "does not have" these tools.

This chapter covers:
- how to open Header and Footer Tools
- different first page
- different headers for different sections
- a practice task: create a different header on the first page only

1) How to Open Header and Footer Tools

To open a header:
1. Double-click at the top of any page (in the header area)
   or
2. Insert tab > Header > choose a header style

To open a footer:
- double-click at the bottom of the page
  or
- Insert tab > Footer

Expected result:
A new contextual tab appears:
- **Header & Footer Tools** (Design)

Beginner rule:
If you do not see Header & Footer Tools, you are not editing the header/footer area.

2) What You Can Do Inside Header & Footer Tools

Common tools you will see:
- Page Number
- Date & Time

- Different First Page
- Different Odd & Even Pages
- Link to Previous
- Go to Header / Go to Footer
- Close Header and Footer

Beginner tip:
Most header problems are caused by sections and "Link to Previous."

3) Different First Page (Most Useful Beginner Feature)
Different First Page lets you have:
- a clean title page with no header

or
- a special header only on page 1

Common use:
- page 1: document title only
- page 2 onward: name + page numbers

Beginner rule:
Use Different First Page for title pages and official documents.

4) Section Differences (When Headers Change Mid-Document)
If your document has sections, each section can have its own header/footer.
This happens when you use:
- section breaks

Key control:
- Link to Previous

If Link to Previous is ON:
- the header/footer matches the previous section

If Link to Previous is OFF:
- you can create a different header/footer for that section

Beginner warning:
People often insert a section break by accident, then wonder why headers change. If headers behave strangely, check for section breaks.

Practice Example (20 to 25 minutes)
Goal: Create a different header on the first page only.

Step 1: Create a two-page document
Open a new document and type:
Title Page
Microsoft Word 2007 Practice Book
Your Name
Now insert a page break:
- Press Ctrl + Enter

Type on page 2:
Chapter 1
This is page 2 content. The header should be different from page 1.

Step 2: Open the header
1. Double-click at the top of page 1
   Header & Footer Tools should appear.

Step 3: Turn on Different First Page
1. In Header & Footer Tools (Design)
2. Check:
   Different First Page

Expected result:
- page 1 header becomes separate
- page 2 and onward share a normal header

Step 4: Create the first page header (or leave it blank)
Option A (common):
Leave page 1 header blank (clean title page)
Option B:
Type a simple title in the first page header:
Microsoft Word 2007 Practice Book

Step 5: Create the header for page 2 and onward
1. Scroll to page 2
2. Click in the header area of page 2 (still in header editing mode)
3. Type something like:
   Your Name | Chapter 1

Step 6: Close the header
1. Click Close Header and Footer
   or
2. Double-click in the main document body

Expected result:
- page 1 header is blank or special
- page 2 header shows the normal header text

Optional: Add page numbers only from page 2
If you want page numbers to start on page 2:
  1. Open header/footer
  2. Insert > Page Number
  3. Format Page Numbers
  4. Choose:
     Start at 1
  5. Make sure Different First Page is ON

Beginner note:
Page numbering options can be confusing with sections. If it gets messy, undo and repeat slowly.

Common beginner problems (quick fixes)
"My header is the same on every page."
Fix:
Turn on Different First Page while editing header.
"I typed on page 1 header but it also appears on page 2."
Fix:
Different First Page is not enabled, or you typed in the normal header area. Enable it, then edit page 1 header separately.
"My header changes randomly later in the document."
Fix:
You may have section breaks. Turn on Show/Hide and look for:
Section Break (Next Page)
Then check Link to Previous in each section header.

Quick check (self-test)
- How do you open Header & Footer Tools?
- What does Different First Page do?
- What is Link to Previous used for?
- What is the most common reason headers change unexpectedly?

PART XII: BEGINNER PROJECTS (REWRITE THE BOOK BY BUILDING REAL DOCUMENTS)

CHAPTER 1: PROJECT 1: A ONE-PAGE LETTER

This project combines the basic skills beginners use most often. By the end, you will have a clean, professional one-page letter with consistent spacing, and a simple header/footer with a page number.

Project goal:
- clean spacing
- header/footer setup
- page number
- keep everything on one page

1) What You Will Build

A one-page letter that includes:
- a title or subject line
- a short body (2 to 4 paragraphs)
- a closing and signature line
- a footer with page number (Page 1 of 1, or just 1)

Beginner rule:
For a one-page letter, simplicity looks more professional than heavy design.

2) Setup (Before You Type)

Step 1: Open a new document
- Start Word 2007
- Click Blank Document

Step 2: Save immediately
- Press Ctrl + S
- Save as:
  One-Page Letter Practice.docx

Beginner rule:
Save early so you do not lose work.

3) Page Setup (Quick and Clean)
1. Page Layout tab
2. Margins:
   Choose Normal (or 1 inch margins)

Optional:
If you need more space to keep it one page:
- choose Narrow margins, but do not go too narrow.

4) Type the Letter (Use This Simple Template)

Type this example letter text (you can change names later):
Your Name
Your Address
City, Country
Phone: _____
Email: _____
Date: February 3, 2026
Recipient Name
Organization Name
Organization Address
City, Country
Subject: Request for Information
Dear Recipient Name,
I am writing to request information about your services. I would like to understand the requirements, the process, and the expected timeline.
Please also share any relevant fees and contact details for the person responsible for follow-up. If there is an application form, kindly tell me where to obtain it.
Thank you for your time and support. I look forward to your response.
Sincerely,
Your Name
Beginner tip:
Keep paragraphs short. One-page letters should be easy to scan.

5) Clean Spacing (Make It Look Professional)

Step 1: Turn on Show/Hide (optional)
- Home tab > Show/Hide (¶)

Step 2: Fix paragraph spacing
1. Select the whole document (Ctrl + A)
2. Page Layout tab > Paragraph group

3. Set:
   Spacing Before: 0 pt
   Spacing After: 6 pt (or 8 pt)

Step 3: Fix line spacing
1. Keep everything selected
2. Home tab > Line Spacing
3. Choose 1.15 (or 1.0 if you want a tighter letter)

Beginner rule:
Do not press Enter many times to create spacing. Use spacing settings.

6) Add a Header or Footer (Simple)

For a one-page letter, you can skip the header and only use a footer with a page number. That is the cleanest beginner option.

Add a footer page number
1. Insert tab
2. Page Number
3. Bottom of Page
4. Choose a simple style (center or right)

Expected result:
A page number appears in the footer.

Beginner tip:
If the page number pushes text onto page 2, reduce spacing after paragraphs or tighten margins slightly.

7) Keep the Letter on One Page (Beginner Fixes)

If your letter becomes two pages:
- reduce spacing after paragraphs (6 pt down to 0 pt)
- reduce line spacing (1.15 down to 1.0)
- shorten one paragraph slightly
- use Normal margins, and only use Narrow if necessary

Beginner rule:
Do not reduce font size too much. Keep it readable (11 or 12 is common).

8) Final Check (Before Printing)

Checklist:
- all paragraphs have consistent spacing
- subject line stands out (bold is enough)

- page number is in the footer
- the letter stays on one page
- spelling check is clean (F7)

Optional:
- Print Preview before printing

Practice Task (15 to 30 minutes)
1. Create the letter using the template above
2. Apply spacing and line spacing settings
3. Add a footer page number
4. Run spelling check (F7)
5. Save and close the file
6. Reopen it to confirm it looks the same

Expected result:
A clean one-page letter you can reuse as a template.

Quick check (self-test)
- Which setting replaces pressing Enter many times: spacing or extra blank lines?
- Where do you add page numbers in Word 2007?
- What is one simple way to keep the letter on one page?
- Why should you save early?

CHAPTER 2: PROJECT 2: A SIMPLE CV

A CV (or resume) is a perfect beginner project because it forces you to use clean formatting. A good CV is not about decoration. It is about consistency, alignment, and easy reading.

Project goal:
- use styles for headings
- keep alignment clean
- build clear sections
- maintain consistent formatting from top to bottom

1) What You Will Build

A one to two-page CV with:
- name and contact block
- professional summary (short)
- skills
- work experience
- education
- optional: certifications, languages, references

Beginner rule:
A clean CV beats a colorful CV.

2) Setup (Before You Type)

Step 1: Open a new document and save it
- Open Word 2007
- Save as:
  Simple CV.docx

Step 2: Set the page and font
1. Page Layout tab > Margins > Normal
2. Home tab > Font:
   Choose a readable font (Calibri, Arial, or Times New Roman)
3. Font size:
   11 (body text)

Beginner rule:
Use one font family for the entire CV.

3) Use Styles for CV Headings (The Clean Method)

Styles keep headings consistent and make your CV easier to update later.

Use:
- Heading 1 for your name (or a custom style if you prefer)
- Heading 2 for section titles (Profile, Skills, Experience, Education)
- Normal for body text

How to apply:
1. Select a heading line
2. Home tab > Styles
3. Choose Heading 2 (for section titles)

Beginner tip:
If Heading styles look too large, you can modify them later, but do not manually format each heading differently.

4) CV Layout Options (Beginner-Friendly)

You have two good beginner options:

Option A: One-column CV (simplest)
- everything aligned left
- clean and easy to maintain

Option B: Two-column header area only
- top section has name on left, contact on right
- rest of CV remains one-column

Beginner rule:
Avoid full two-column CV layouts unless you are very comfortable with tables.

5) The Best Beginner Trick: Use a Table for Alignment (Not Spaces)

Beginners often try to align dates and text using spaces. That breaks easily.

Use a table instead:
- a 2-column table with invisible borders can align content perfectly.

Example:
- left column: job title and organization
- right column: dates

Beginner rule:
Do not align using multiple spaces. Use a table or tabs.

Practice Example (30 to 60 minutes)

Goal: Create a simple CV using styles, sections, and consistent formatting.

Step 1: Type your CV content using this structure

[Your Name]

[Phone] | [Email] | [City, Country] | [LinkedIn or Website if you have]

Profile

A short 2 to 3 sentence summary of who you are and what you can do.

Skills

- Skill 1
- Skill 2
- Skill 3
- Skill 4

Work Experience

Job Title, Organization

City, Country | Month Year to Month Year

- Achievement or responsibility
- Achievement or responsibility
- Achievement or responsibility

Education

Degree, School

City, Country | Year

- Optional short detail

Certifications (Optional)

- Certification name, year

Languages (Optional)

- Language: level

References (Optional)

Available upon request.

Step 2: Apply styles to section headings

Select each section title and apply:

- Heading 2

Example section titles:

- Profile
- Skills
- Work Experience
- Education

Keep body text as Normal.

Step 3: Make headings consistent

Do not change each heading manually. If headings look too big:
1. Right-click Heading 2 in Styles
2. Modify
3. Choose:
   Font size 12 or 13, bold
4. OK

Now all headings update together.

Step 4: Clean alignment for dates (use a simple table)

For each job entry, create a 2-column table with 1 row:
Left cell:
Job Title, Organization
Right cell:
Dates
How:
1. Insert tab > Table > 2 columns x 1 row
2. Type job details
3. Select the table
4. Table Tools > Design > Borders > No Border
5. Align right cell text to the right:
   Table Tools > Layout > Align Right

Repeat for education entries if needed.
Beginner tip:
This creates professional alignment without fighting spacing.

Step 5: Keep spacing consistent
1. Select the whole document (Ctrl + A)
2. Page Layout tab > Spacing:
   Before: 0 pt
   After: 6 pt
3. Home tab > Line spacing:
   1.0 or 1.15

Then check sections:
- headings may need slightly more space before them (optional)

6) Final CV Cleanup Checklist

Check:
- one font family used
- consistent font sizes (name is larger, headings slightly larger, body is normal)

- headings are styled, not manually formatted
- bullet points are consistent
- dates align neatly (table method or tab stops)
- no extra blank lines created by repeated Enter presses
- spelling is clean (F7)

Practice Task (What to Deliver)
1. Build the CV using the structure above
2. Apply Heading 2 to all section titles
3. Use the 2-column borderless table method for dates
4. Standardize spacing across the document
5. Save, close, and reopen to confirm everything stayed consistent

Expected result:
A clean CV template you can update anytime without fighting formatting.

Common beginner problems (quick fixes)
"My headings look different from each other."
Fix:
Use Heading 2 style everywhere. Do not format headings manually.
"My dates do not line up."
Fix:
Use a borderless 2-column table or tab stops. Do not use spaces.
"My CV looks too long."
Fix:
Shorten bullet points and remove repeated phrases. Keep only the strongest items.

Quick check (self-test)
- Why are styles better than manual formatting for CV headings?
- What is the safest way to align dates: spaces, tabs, or a borderless table?
- Which two spacing settings make a CV look consistent?
- What is the first thing you should do before heavy formatting?

CHAPTER 3: PROJECT 3: A SCHOOL REPORT

This project teaches beginners how to build a real school report that looks organized and academic. You will use headings, generate a table of contents, and practice simple citations and a bibliography.

Project goal:
- headings that structure the report
- table of contents that updates
- basic citations
- bibliography generation

1) What You Will Build

A 3 to 5 page school report with:
- title page
- headings and subheadings
- table of contents
- at least 2 citations
- a bibliography at the end

Beginner rule:
A report becomes easy when headings and styles are used correctly.

2) Setup (Before You Type)

Step 1: Create a new document and save it
Save as:
School Report Project.docx

Step 2: Set clean page layout
- Page Layout > Margins > Normal
- Font: readable (Calibri or Times New Roman)
- Font size: 11 or 12 for body text

Step 3: Plan your report sections
A simple beginner structure:
- Introduction
- Main Section 1
- Main Section 2
- Conclusion
- References / Bibliography

3) Apply Headings the Right Way (Key Skill)

Use Styles, not manual formatting.
Use:
- Heading 1 for main sections (Introduction, Conclusion)
- Heading 2 for sub-sections (Background, Findings)

How:
1. Type the heading text
2. Select it
3. Home tab > Styles > Heading 1 or Heading 2

Beginner rule:
If you want a Table of Contents, you must use heading styles.

4) Insert a Table of Contents (TOC)

Before inserting TOC:
- make sure headings are styled (Heading 1, Heading 2)

How to insert TOC:
1. Put your cursor where the TOC should go (usually after title page)
2. References tab
3. Table of Contents
4. Choose an automatic style

How to update TOC:
1. Click inside the TOC
2. Update Table
3. Choose:
- update page numbers only, or
- update entire table (best after edits)

Beginner tip:
If the TOC looks wrong, your headings are not applied correctly.

5) Add Citations and Bibliography (Beginner Level)

Word 2007 can store sources and generate a bibliography.

Add a source
1. References tab
2. Insert Citation
3. Add New Source
4. Choose source type (Book, Website, Journal Article)
5. Fill in basic details
6. OK

Insert a citation
- References tab > Insert Citation
- choose the source you saved

Insert a bibliography
1. Place cursor at end of document
2. References tab
3. Bibliography
4. Choose a style (Bibliography or Works Cited)

Beginner rule:
Use Word's tool so formatting stays consistent.

Practice Example (45 to 90 minutes)
Goal: Create a simple school report with headings, TOC, citations, and a bibliography.

Step 1: Build the document structure
Page 1: Title page
School Report Title
Your Name
Class / Subject
Teacher Name
Date
Insert a page break (Ctrl + Enter)
Page 2: Table of Contents page
Type:
Table of Contents
Press Enter, then insert TOC there later.
Insert a page break (Ctrl + Enter)
Now start the report content.

Step 2: Add headings and sample content
Heading 1: Introduction
Write 1 to 2 short paragraphs.
Heading 1: Background
Heading 2: Key Concepts
Write a short paragraph.
Heading 1: Discussion
Heading 2: Evidence or Examples
Write 2 short paragraphs.
Heading 1: Conclusion
Write 1 short paragraph.

Heading 1: Bibliography
Leave it blank for now.
Important:
Apply Heading styles to every heading.

Step 3: Add two sources and citations
Add Source 1 (example book):
- References > Insert Citation > Add New Source
- Type: Book
- Fill in:

  Author, Title, Year, City, Publisher

Insert the citation in your Discussion section.
Add Source 2 (example website):
- References > Insert Citation > Add New Source
- Type: Website
- Fill in:

  Author (if available), Name of Web Page, Year, URL, Access date (if prompted)

Insert the citation in your Background or Discussion section.
Beginner note:
If you do not have real sources now, use practice entries. The goal is learning the tool steps.

Step 4: Insert the bibliography
1. Go to the Bibliography section at the end
2. References tab > Bibliography
3. Choose Bibliography

Word generates the list automatically.

Step 5: Insert and update the Table of Contents
1. Go back to the Table of Contents page
2. Click under the heading "Table of Contents"
3. References tab > Table of Contents > choose an automatic style

After that:
- edit your report and then update the TOC:
  - click the TOC > Update Table > Update entire table

Expected result:
Your TOC lists headings and correct page numbers.

Final Report Checklist
Check:

- headings use Heading 1 and Heading 2 styles
- TOC generates from headings
- citations appear inside your text
- bibliography appears at the end
- spacing is consistent across the document
- no extra blank lines are used for spacing
- spelling check is clean (F7)

Common beginner problems (quick fixes)
"My Table of Contents is missing headings."
Fix:
You did not apply Heading styles. Apply Heading 1 and Heading 2, then update TOC.
"My bibliography is empty."
Fix:
You inserted a bibliography before adding sources. Add sources first, then insert or update bibliography.
"My citations look wrong."
Fix:
Check the selected citation style in References tab (APA, MLA, etc.). Choose the style your teacher requires.

Quick check (self-test)
- Why must you use Heading styles for a TOC?
- Where do you insert citations?
- Where do you generate a bibliography?
- What does "Update entire table" do in the TOC?

CHAPTER 4: PROJECT 4: A FLYER OR ANNOUNCEMENT

This project helps beginners create a simple flyer that looks clean and professional without complicated design. You will use a picture, a text box, and one or two shapes. The main skill is layout control.

Project goal:
- insert and control a picture
- use a text box for clean positioning
- add a simple shape (optional)
- keep the layout neat and readable

1) What You Will Build

A one-page flyer with:
- a bold title
- a short message (what, when, where, contact)
- one picture
- one callout or highlight box (optional)

Beginner rule:
A good flyer is readable in 5 seconds.

2) Setup (Before You Design)

Step 1: Create a new document and save it
Save as:
Flyer Project.docx
Step 2: Choose a page orientation
Go to:
- Page Layout tab > Orientation

Choose:
- Portrait (most flyers)
  or
- Landscape (if your design needs more width)

Beginner tip:
Portrait is easier for beginners.
Step 3: Set margins
- Page Layout > Margins > Narrow (optional)
  Use Narrow only if you need more space. Keep safe space around edges.

3) The Beginner Layout Method (Safe and Clean)

Use these building blocks:

- Title at the top (normal text, large and bold)
- A picture under or beside the title
- A text box for the main details
- Optional shape for a highlight (like "Free Entry")

Beginner rule:
Do not use many fonts. Use one font family and two sizes (title and body).

4) Insert and Control the Picture

Step 1: Insert a picture
- Insert tab > Picture > choose an image

Step 2: Set Wrap Text to control it
1. Click the picture
2. Picture Tools > Format
3. Text Wrapping > Square

Step 3: Resize correctly
- drag a corner handle to resize (avoid distortion)

Step 4: Position it
- drag to place it where it supports the flyer

Beginner tip:
If the picture fights you, switch to Square wrapping and try again.

5) Add a Text Box for the Details

Text boxes are the easiest way to place text exactly where you want.
1. Insert tab > Text Box
2. Draw a box under the title or beside the picture
3. Type the key details inside:

What:
When:
Where:
Contact:

Format it:
- use bold for labels (What, When, Where)
- keep body size 11 or 12
- align left for readability

Clean it:
- Drawing Tools > Format
- Shape Fill: white or very light gray

- Shape Outline: light gray or no outline

Beginner rule:
Text box should help clarity, not decorate.

6) Optional: Add a Simple Callout Shape (One Only)
Example callout text:
- FREE ENTRY
- ALL ARE WELCOME
- LIMITED SEATS

How:
1. Insert tab > Shapes
2. Choose a simple shape (rectangle or callout)
3. Type text inside
4. Format:
- light fill color
- simple outline
- bold text

Beginner rule:
One callout is enough. Too many makes the flyer look noisy.

Practice Example (45 to 60 minutes)
Goal: Create a clean flyer using a picture, a text box, and optional shape.

Step 1: Type the flyer title
At the top of the page, type:
Community Training Announcement
Format the title:
- font size 24 to 32
- bold
- center (optional)

Step 2: Insert a picture
Insert tab > Picture
Then:
- Picture Tools > Format > Wrap Text > Square
- Resize to medium size
- Place it near the top, below the title, or to the side

Step 3: Insert a text box for details
Insert tab > Text Box
Draw it below the picture or beside it.
Type:

Topic: Microsoft Word 2007 for Beginners
Date: February 10, 2026
Time: 10:00 AM to 12:00 PM
Venue: Community Hall
Entry: Free
Contact: Your Phone Number
Format:
- bold the labels (Topic, Date, Time, Venue, Entry, Contact)
- keep spacing consistent

Step 4: Add an optional callout

Insert > Shapes > choose a simple callout or rectangle
Type:
FREE ENTRY
Format:
- Shape Fill: light color
- Outline: dark or none
- Text: bold, large enough to notice

Step 5: Align everything neatly

Use:
- Picture Tools > Align
- Drawing Tools > Align
    Or manual alignment with careful dragging.

Beginner checklist:
- no overlapping objects
- enough white space
- text is readable
- one main message, not many competing items

Step 6: Save and print preview

1. Save
2. Print Preview
3. Check margins and cutoffs
4. Adjust positions if needed

Expected result:
A clean one-page flyer that prints well.

Common beginner problems (quick fixes)

"My text moves around when I drag the picture."
Fix:
Set Wrap Text to Square for the picture and text box.

"Objects overlap and I cannot select the one underneath."
Fix:
Use:
- Home tab > Select (if available)
  or
- temporarily move the top object
  Also consider:
- Bring Forward / Send Backward under Drawing Tools

"The flyer looks crowded."
Fix:
Remove one element, reduce text, increase white space.

Quick check (self-test)
- What wrap setting is best for beginners when placing pictures?
- Why use a text box instead of typing everything normally?
- What makes a flyer readable quickly?
- What is the biggest beginner mistake in flyer design?

CHAPTER 5: TROUBLESHOOTING CLINIC

This chapter is your "first aid" section. When beginners get stuck in Word 2007, the problem is usually one of a few common issues. The fastest way to fix Word problems is to identify the type of problem, then apply the correct simple fix. This chapter covers fast fixes for:

- spacing problems
- page numbers problems
- images that move or jump
- broken bullets and numbering
- Table of Contents (TOC) not updating

1) Spacing Problems (The Most Common)
Problem A: Big gaps between paragraphs
Cause:

- extra blank lines (many paragraph marks)
or
- paragraph spacing (Before/After) set too high

Fast fix:
1. Turn on Show/Hide (Home tab > ¶)
2. If you see many ¶ marks, delete extras
3. Select all (Ctrl + A)
4. Page Layout tab > Paragraph spacing:
   Before: 0 pt
   After: 6 pt (or 0 pt for tight documents)

Beginner rule:
Use paragraph spacing settings, not repeated Enter presses.

Problem B: Double spaces between words
Cause:

- pressing Spacebar twice

Fast fix:
1. Ctrl + H
2. Find:
   (two spaces)
3. Replace:
   (one space)
4. Replace All
   Repeat until Word finds 0 matches.

Problem C: Text is not aligned even though it "looks aligned"

Cause:
- manual alignment using spaces or tabs inconsistently

Fast fix:
- remove extra spaces
- use a table for alignment, or set tab stops

2) Page Number Problems

Problem A: Page numbers start on the title page but you want them to start on page 2

Fast fix (simple method):
1. Open header/footer (double-click top or bottom)
2. Turn on:
   Different First Page
3. Delete page number from page 1 header/footer
4. Keep page number on page 2 and onward

Problem B: Wrong page number format (Roman numerals, etc.)

Fast fix:
1. Insert tab > Page Number > Format Page Numbers
2. Choose number format (1, 2, 3)
3. Choose:
   Continue from previous section
   or Start at 1 (depending on your goal)

Problem C: Page numbers change unexpectedly mid-document

Cause:
- section breaks + Link to Previous settings

Fast fix:
1. Turn on Show/Hide (¶)
2. Look for Section Break (Next Page)
3. Open header/footer in the section where the problem starts
4. Turn Link to Previous OFF if you want a different header/footer
   or keep it ON if you want the same numbering and header/footer

Beginner rule:
Most page number confusion is actually a section break problem.

3) Images Moving, Jumping, or Refusing to Stay Put

Problem A: You cannot move the picture freely

Cause:
- picture is In Line with Text

Fast fix:
1. Click the picture
2. Picture Tools > Format
3. Wrap Text > Square
   Now drag it into position.

Problem B: Picture jumps when you type

Cause:
- wrapping and anchor behavior

Fast fix (beginner safe method):
1. Wrap Text > Square
2. Keep the picture near the paragraph it belongs to
3. Avoid Behind Text and In Front of Text

Problem C: Text overlaps the picture

Fast fix:
1. Wrap Text > Square
2. Move the picture slightly away
3. If needed, use:
   Wrap Text > More Layout Options and increase distance from text

Beginner rule:
Square wrapping solves most picture problems.

4) Broken Lists (Bullets and Numbering)

Problem A: Numbering restarts at 1 when you do not want it to

Fast fix:
1. Click inside the numbered list
2. Right-click the number
3. Choose:
   Continue Numbering

Problem B: Numbering will not restart at 1 when you want it to

Fast fix:
1. Right-click the number you want to restart
2. Choose:
   Restart at 1

Problem C: Bullets and numbering become mixed and messy
Cause:
- manual changes, copy/paste from the web, inconsistent styles

Fast fix:
1. Select the messy list
2. Home tab > Clear Formatting
3. Reapply bullets or numbering fresh

Beginner rule:
If a list becomes stubborn, clear formatting and rebuild it.

5) TOC Not Updating (Table of Contents Problems)
Problem A: Headings do not appear in TOC
Cause:
- you typed headings manually (bold/large) but did not apply Heading styles

Fast fix:
1. Select each heading
2. Apply:
Heading 1 or Heading 2 from Styles
3. Click the TOC
4. Update Table > Update entire table

Problem B: Page numbers in TOC are wrong
Cause:
- content moved, but TOC not updated

Fast fix:
- Click TOC > Update Table > Update page numbers only

Problem C: TOC looks strange or includes wrong items
Cause:
- wrong styles used for headings, or accidental heading style on normal text

Fast fix:
1. Turn on Show/Hide
2. Click suspicious lines and check the style name
3. Change body text back to Normal
4. Update TOC again

Beginner rule:
A TOC is only as good as your heading styles.

Quick "Diagnosis" Checklist (Use This Every Time)
If something looks wrong, ask:
- Is it a spacing problem?
- Is it a section break problem?
- Is it a wrapping problem (pictures/objects)?
- Is it a style problem (headings/lists)?
- Did I copy/paste messy text from the web?

Then apply the matching fix above.

Practice Mini-Clinic (30 to 45 minutes)
Goal: Practice fixing the five most common issues.
1. Create a messy paragraph with extra spaces and blank lines
2. Fix it using Show/Hide and Replace
3. Insert page numbers and make the first page different
4. Insert a picture and set Wrap Text to Square
5. Create a numbered list and force it to restart and continue
6. Create headings and insert a TOC, then update it after changes

Expected result:
You can quickly diagnose and fix common Word problems without panic.

Quick check (self-test)
- What tool reveals hidden paragraph marks and spaces?
- What wrap setting solves most image problems?
- What causes page numbering to change in the middle of a document?
- Why do TOC problems usually happen?
- What is your fastest reset when formatting becomes messy?

BACK MATTER

Back Matter 1: Keyboard Shortcuts Cheat Sheet

These shortcuts save time and reduce mistakes. Practice them until they feel natural.

File and basic actions
- Ctrl + N: New document
- Ctrl + O: Open
- Ctrl + S: Save
- F12: Save As
- Ctrl + P: Print
- Ctrl + W: Close document

Editing and selection
- Ctrl + A: Select all
- Ctrl + C: Copy
- Ctrl + X: Cut
- Ctrl + V: Paste
- Ctrl + Z: Undo
- Ctrl + Y: Redo
- Ctrl + F: Find
- Ctrl + H: Find and Replace

Formatting
- Ctrl + B: Bold
- Ctrl + I: Italic
- Ctrl + U: Underline
- Ctrl + Shift + > : Increase font size
- Ctrl + Shift + < : Decrease font size
- Ctrl + Spacebar: Clear character formatting (reset font styling)
- Ctrl + Q: Clear paragraph formatting (reset paragraph styling)

Paragraph and page control
- Enter: New paragraph
- Shift + Enter: Line break (new line without new paragraph)
- Ctrl + Enter: Page break
- Ctrl + 1: Single line spacing
- Ctrl + 2: Double line spacing
- Ctrl + 5: 1.5 line spacing

Review and navigation

- F7: Spelling and Grammar
- Ctrl + Home: Go to start of document
- Ctrl + End: Go to end of document
- Ctrl + Left Arrow / Right Arrow: Jump by words
- Ctrl + Up Arrow / Down Arrow: Jump by paragraphs
- Ctrl + Mouse Wheel: Zoom in/out

Tables (useful basics)
- Tab (in a table cell): Move to next cell
- Shift + Tab (in a table cell): Move to previous cell

Beginner tip:
If you remember only five shortcuts, start with:
Ctrl + S, Ctrl + Z, Ctrl + C, Ctrl + V, Ctrl + H

Back Matter 2: Glossary of Key Word 2007 Terms

Ribbon
The top command area with tabs and groups of tools.

Tab
A category on the Ribbon (Home, Insert, Page Layout, References, Mailings, Review, View).

Group
A cluster of related tools on a tab (example: Font group, Paragraph group).

Dialog Box Launcher
A small arrow in a group that opens more detailed settings.

Office Button
The round button in the top-left (Word 2007). It contains Open, Save, Print, and options.

Quick Access Toolbar
Small toolbar near the Office Button. You can add Save, Undo, Redo, and other frequent commands.

Status Bar
Bottom bar showing page number, word count, and view/zoom controls.

Document Area
The main area where you type and edit.

Cursor (Insertion Point)
The blinking line showing where text will appear.

Selection
Highlighted text that will be edited, copied, formatted, or deleted.

Clipboard
Temporary storage for cut or copied content.
Paste Options
Choices after pasting (keep formatting, match destination, keep text only).
Formatting
Changing how text looks (font, size, bold, spacing, alignment).
Paragraph Formatting
Changes that affect a paragraph (alignment, indentation, spacing, line spacing).
Style
A saved set of formatting you apply with one click (Heading 1, Heading 2, Normal).
Show/Hide Marks (¶)
Displays hidden marks such as paragraph breaks, spaces, and tabs.
Page Break
Forces the next text to start on a new page (Ctrl + Enter).
Section Break
Splits the document into sections so parts can have different headers, footers, and page numbering.
Header and Footer
Top and bottom areas of pages used for titles, names, and page numbers.
Track Changes
Records edits so you can accept or reject them.
Comments
Notes attached to text for feedback without changing the text.
Table of Contents (TOC)
An automatic list of headings with page numbers, built from heading styles.
Mail Merge
Creates many letters/labels using one template and a recipient list.
Contextual Tabs
Tabs that appear only when you select an object (Picture Tools, Table Tools, Drawing Tools).

Back Matter 3: Skills Checklist (What You Should Now Be Able To Do)

Use this list to confirm you are ready to use Word 2007 confidently.

Quick start skills
- Open Word and identify the main screen parts
- Create, save, reopen, and print a document safely
- Use Print Preview to avoid wasting paper

Writing and editing skills
- Type, select text, and move the cursor using mouse and keyboard
- Use Undo and Redo to fix mistakes fast
- Cut, copy, paste, and choose paste options correctly
- Use Find and Replace safely

Formatting skills
- Format text with fonts, size, bold, italic, underline, and color
- Format paragraphs with alignment, spacing, indentation, and line spacing
- Create bullets and numbered lists, restart and continue numbering
- Apply styles (Heading 1, Heading 2) to structure documents
- Use Format Painter and Clear Formatting to fix messy text

Page layout skills
- Set margins, orientation, and paper size
- Insert page breaks and understand section breaks
- Add headers, footers, and page numbers
- Create simple columns and use page background tools carefully

Insert skills
- Insert and format pictures with wrapping and cropping
- Create simple shapes, text boxes, and callouts
- Create and format tables (borders, shading, alignment, simple sort)
- Insert SmartArt and simple charts
- Insert common symbols

Academic and long-document skills
- Use headings to navigate long documents

- Create and update a table of contents
- Insert footnotes and basic citations
- Generate a bibliography
- Add captions and cross-references (basic use)

Review and collaboration skills
- Run spelling and grammar checks wisely
- Add comments for feedback
- Use Track Changes and accept/reject edits
- Compare two versions of a document
- Protect a document with basic restrictions

View and navigation skills
- Switch views (Print Layout, Draft, Web Layout, Outline, Reading)
- Use zoom, split view, and side-by-side reading tools
- Use Show/Hide marks to fix spacing and formatting problems

Project skills
- Build a one-page letter with clean spacing and page number
- Create a simple CV with consistent headings and alignment
- Build a school report with headings, TOC, citations, and bibliography
- Create a clean flyer using pictures and text boxes
- Diagnose and fix common Word problems quickly

If you can do most items above without looking up steps, you are ready.

REVIEWS
If this book helped you learn Microsoft Word 2007, please leave a short review on Amazon.
A good review can be simple. You can mention:
- who you are (student, office worker, teacher, beginner)
- what you used the book for (letters, CV, school report, church/office documents)
- one chapter or project that helped you most
- what changed for you after practicing (speed, confidence, cleaner documents)

Even a few sentences help other beginners choose the right book.

HOW TO ORDER COPIES
If you want printed copies for a school, office, church, NGO, or training program, you can order in bulk.
Bulk orders are useful for:
- computer classes and labs
- staff training
- student training programs
- community training and workshops

To request bulk orders or training-use copies, contact:
- Email: maluthabiel@gmail.com
- Website: www.johnshalom.com
- Phone/WhatsApp: +211 927 145 394

When you write, include:
- how many copies you need
- the country and city for delivery
- whether you want a standard order or training packs

ABOUT THE AUTHOR

John Monyjok Maluth is a writer, teacher, and coach focused on practical learning and human growth. He writes beginner-friendly guides that help readers move from confusion to competence through simple steps and real practice.
He works in ICT and communication, and he believes digital skills should be clear, usable, and available to ordinary people, not only experts.

Website: www.johnshalom.com
Email: maluthabiel@gmail.com

www.ingramcontent.com/pod-product-compliance
Lightning Source LLC
Chambersburg PA
CBHW020901180526
45163CB00007B/2584